Whenever there is cultural dec
"crying in the wilderness," so
the good in society. Such a voi
mid-nineteenth century. His w ....
them in this translation, I felt that, details apart, Groen was talking about the cultural and moral situation in our world, including here in Canada. C.S. Lewis and C.K. Chesterton would have agreed with much of what Groen wrote before their time, if they had had this translation. Boersma has therefore done us a service bringing Groen's concerns and thoughts to English speakers.

Ed & Annette Norman
PhD & BSc
Kemptville, ON

Groen van Prinsterer's knowledge of the Bible and history, as well as his logic, demonstrates how the awareness of God and His sovereignty is tantamount to a nation's blessing and survival. While most of his writings were recorded some 150 years ago, his works provide relevant and important insight today. His writing makes it clear that there are only two sides to the world's culture war: those who deny God and put the self in His place, and those who submit to the authority of He who created all things, and subjugate themselves to that authority. The compiler of Van Prinsterer's writings (Smitskamp) and Harmen Boersma's work of translating are to be commended for helping to bring this invaluable understanding to the English-speaking world.

Dean Brdlik
Southern Baptist Senior Pastor
Lewisburg, WV

"A nation is...more than an incidental gathering of individuals; rather it is the result of historic development that shapes its unique character, distinguishable from all other nations. What is a nation...when one destroys the continuation of the unity of history, religion, traditions, customs and principles from ancestors to descendants?" Although Groen van Prinsterer lived in nineteenth-century Netherlands, his thoughts on the roles of Christian faith, Christian schools, the state, history and tradition could well apply to Canada today.

Marie Cooper
Christian school board member
Ottawa, ON

Not having been previously aware of Groen, I found a timeless quality in the description of his belief. I was particularly interested in how he differentiated what he believed to be the only two political worldviews. In modern politics, we are fragmented on the left-right axis initially defined during the French Revolution—but Groen's notion that reactionary and revolutionary politics were actually two heads of the same worldview—in contrast to the "Christian Historic"—was a unique perspective I had not previously considered. Clearly Groen shared with Burke the belief in the supremacy of God and the imperative of respecting the wisdom of our ancestors. Modern audiences would do well to heed his advice to respect our history and institutions.

John Whittaker
Political Policy Analyst
Calgary, AB

We have gone through a revolution in modern times where the laws of God have been replaced by human arbitrariness. Van Prinsterer observes that this revolution has never been able to provide what it promises. Only when we recognize the causes of our problems will we be able to do anything to correct them. It will be a challenge for us to discover the principles on which our country was founded. These have been essentially left out of contemporary writing. It could prove to be of great profit to dig out the less accessible materials of the past to demonstrate our roots. The book is a challenging and profitable read.

James W. Reaves
Reformed Pastor Emeritus
Kelowna, BC

I found this book about Groen van Prinsterer very interesting. I am reading it from my perspective as a Westerner, as I have never lived in Europe. Even though his books and his life occur in the 1800s, they are as up to date as if written in our modern times.

Ruth Shurtliff
Federal government employee (retired)
Ottawa, ON

Dutch historian and politician Groen van Prinsterer provides an example for both elected politicians and conscientious citizens to put principle ahead of party. Harmen Boersma's translation of Hendrik Smitskamp's Building a Nation on Rock or Sand: Groen van Prinsterer for Today *is an excellent introduction to his life and ideas, which found no compromise with the revolutionary spirit and results of modernity. Van Prinsterer warns both the public official and citizen against not only unbelief but the trap of fallacies of a "stretched, shaped and softened" Christian teaching.*

Paul Tuns
Newspaper Editor
Toronto, ON

Groen was a nineteenth-century Netherlandic patriot who was engaged in the politics of his day, serving the parliament of the Netherlands and offering a conservative solution to the problems of the day. He felt that the key to ultimate positive and beneficial change in society was to be based on a proper understanding of the principles to be found in Scripture. Certain principles that uphold freedom of conscience, freedom of religious worship and parental rights in education are scripture based and are worthy of study and emulation. There are a lot of good questions included in the final pages that could be helpful in the application of these ideas to the Canadian experience.

Dan DiRocco
high school principal (retired)
Editorial Advisory Board member, *The Interim*
Toronto, ON

For those interested in the intersection of faith and politics, this book makes a useful contribution. The life and works of Groen van Prinsterer provide an understanding of how Christians have wrestled with applying the teachings of Christ to the politics of their time. While van Prinsterer may have lived in a different era, he dealt with issues that have strong parallels to today. Seeing how he handled the politics of his day provides guidance for Christians now.

Brad Trost
Member of Parliament
Saskatoon, SK

The revolutionary idea—that authority is arbitrary as opposed to God-given—is one that Groen van Prinsterer fought and wrote against with clarity of mind. A timely topic, because we also live in a time when authority is questioned and we need to know why government is more than the collective will of the people. This book is a worthwhile look back at history and political principles in nineteenth-century Netherlands. It can also be read simply for edification: "The Lord does not need our participation to be victorious but desires it." Encouraging words from a great man! Groen van Prinsterer lived out his faith in his time—let us do likewise!

Peter Vogel
Deputy Leader political party
Ottawa, ON

As a citizen of both Canada and the Netherlands without a working knowledge of the Dutch language, I read Harmen Boersma's translation of Dr. Smitskamp's Building a Nation ... with great interest. I knew of Guillaume Groen van Prinsterer's thoughtful influence on Abraham Kuyper, but this work—thanks to extended topically arranged quotations—makes his ideas directly accessible. That it appears in the sesquicentennial of the Canadian Confederation—which occurred during Van Prinsterer's lifetime—is particularly timely. While Canadian readers will recognize differences in context from our present circumstances, Van Prinsterer's principled approach to political thought provides ample basis for reflection. The attentive reader will be educated in Netherlandic history and challenged by Van Prinsterer's convictions. Readers who simplistically identify with either the conservative or liberal side of contemporary political and religious divides will be challenged by Van Prinsterer's view of their common roots in "revolutionary thought" and pressed to consider alternatives, centred on the gospel in word and action, which "holds the true principles of freedom, equality, brotherhood, philanthropy and beneficial humanitarianism." The final section—Groen's Specific Examples—in particular, delineates Van Prinsterer's foundational thought in detail. The discerning reader may be uncomfortable with Van Prinsterer's monarchial nationalism but may carefully consider his thoughts on freedom, responsibility, partisanship, incrementalism, tolerance, compromise and unity. Mr. Boersma has done a great service to the thoughtful Christian by publishing this work in English.

Jacob Zwiers
Christian school board chair
Ottawa, ON

The many direct quotes from the "anti-revolutionary" politician describe his efforts to restore Biblical values in the Netherlands in the 1800s. His clear insight into the reasons why unbelief and humanistic rebellion against Christian principles are so strong is helpful to us today...Most encouraging among Groen van Prinsterer's frequently recurring themes are the reminders to Christians of our duty to persist, even when the battle seems hopeless and the cause lost. Canadian Christians of all ethnic descent will gain from a reading and application of the principles found in this little book. A few of my favourite nuggets are these:

"...discouragement does not behoove the Netherlander nor the Christian. When persuasion seems impossible, witnessing remains a duty."

"[Even] under unfavourable circumstances, truthful witnessing can continue. This ongoing witness is a powerful practice in itself. The preaching of the truth is not redundant during times of unrighteousness."

"An irresistible flow of events does not remove personal responsibility. Nobody needs to bend the knee for the idol of the age. One will not be judged for the impossibility of resistance but rather for the willingness to cooperate."

"A religious conviction loses its power when it does not, in support of that which it confesses as truth, use the means available in the interest of church and state."

"Parents who by intuition or well-founded argument in their conscience are convinced that the character of education in the existing educational system is unchristian should not be prevented from offering their children an education consistent with their conscience before God."

Rod Taylor
National Leader political party
Ottawa, ON

Building a Nation on Rock or Sand

Groen Van Prinsterer for Today

By H. Smitskamp
Translated and Edited by Harmen Boersma

Belleville, Ontario, Canada

To order additional copies, visit:
www.essencebookstore.com

Every effort has been made to track the copyright status of the original document. This translation has been published following the European Orphan Works Directive, which was implemented in the Netherlands in 2014. In acknowledgment of Dr. Smitskamp's Christian vision throughout his lifetime of research and writing, an amount equivalent to copyright payments for the Netherlandic work will be donated to Cardus, 185 Young Street, Hamilton, ON, L8N 1V9 (905-528-8866). Inquiries may be directed there.

Cover photo courtesy of Kira Lodder & The Cardus Think Tank

Guardian Books is an imprint of *Essence Publishing,* a Christian Book Publisher dedicated to furthering the work of Christ through the written word. For more information, contact:
20 Hanna Court, Belleville, Ontario, Canada K8P 5J2
Phone: 1-800-238-6376 • Fax: (613) 962-3055
Email: info@essence-publishing.com
Web site: www.essence-publishing.com

Printed in Canada
by

Guardian
B O O K S

Dedicated to Canadians
as a gift on their
sesquicentennial celebration
and to citizens in every
nation of the world

"Therefore, whoever hears these sayings of Mine, and does them, I will liken him to a wise man who built his house on the rock: and the rain descended, and the floods came, and the winds blew and beat on that house, and it did not fall, for it was founded on the rock. But everyone who hears these sayings of Mine, and does not do them, will be like a foolish man who built his house on the sand: and the rain descended, the floods came, and the winds blew and beat on that house; and it fell. And great was its fall" (Matthew 7:24-27 NKJV; spoken by Jesus to His disciples and the multitude in the Sermon on the Mount).

Acknowledgement

A pre-publication e-book of *Building a Nation…* was sent to a limited number of interested citizens in Canada and the United States. You just read their summarized comments. My sincere gratitude is due them for their thoughtful observations and kind permission to include them. The final translation and the edited context remain my responsibility. Their feedback gauged the initial reception of *Groen van Prinsterer for Today* in the twenty-first century. All other feedback from spouse, family, relatives, friends, and acquaintances have greatly enlarged the audience and purpose of this edition. Thank you! *Soli Deo Gloria*.

Contents

APPENDIX

Introduction

A yellowed copy of Dr. Hendrik Smitskamp's book arrived in our mailbox early 2000. The box also contained three titles by Dr. Abraham Kuyper and a few by other well-known theologians of the period. These books had belonged to my late parents, Gerrit and Sibrigje Boersma. "These are a few of their valued belongings worth sending across the ocean to their only Canadian son," Piet, the executor-brother had decided.

I remember as a boy seeing books, all neatly covered with brown packing paper, tightly lined up on the top shelf of the cupboard in the only heated living room of our parental home, the dairy farm house in Allingawier, Friesland. The late parents of my spouse, Elizabeth, Harm and Jantje Bouwman, who farmed near Twijzel, Friesland, had their book-packed cupboard in the living room, too. Two Reformed confessing families eking out a livelihood with their independent business and living their rural lifestyle, tied in with church, community and nation.

Every once in a while, Dad would take a book down and read in it. He may have been challenged as the chair of the church council or as a board member of the village Christian-national school or the Christian farmers organization. [Possibly the regional Anti-Revolutionary party meeting had piqued his interest in a topic or political decision.] Early on, I was the silent, playing participant in conversations with relatives, visitors or neighbours around the dining room table. However, I cannot recall Dad introducing the authors to me. He left that up to the teachers of the local Christian schools I attended later.

Curious, I immediately read Smitskamp's linen-bound copy. It stirred my memory of growing up in this more than a millennium old, rural, mixed-faith community spurred on by thinkers like Groen van Prinsterer and Abraham Kuyper. As others might benefit from Groen's ideas summarized in Smitskamp's concise volume if it were available in English, here it is!

Smitskamp explains his intent of this publication himself: "Don't look for a complete picture of Groen's teachings nor his works. Nor a critical treatment of his ideas concerning various topics. We are interested in understanding his reply to the questions of *our* times; his warnings against dangers that he foresaw and predicted; and his pointers to the calling of the (Netherlandic) Christian living among these dangers...This approach means that quotes will be plentiful. No apology for that. My task is limited to arranging his quoted ideas in a coherent presentation, and with as little historical explanation as possible. *We are interested in Groen's thoughts*, not in our thoughts of Groen."[1]

To honour Smitskamp's intent in the English text, you will notice that it has been written as a continuous story in which two writers blend into one. Smitskamp writes his own text and includes Groen's selections in quotation marks. These have not been blocked and indented on purpose. The two texts read smoothly from one to the other, back and forth posing the same challenge.

The epilogue has been added in this English translation to facilitate thoughtful reflection and stimulate group discussion. Their study and application is a way to increase meaningful participation in society.

Groen van Prinsterer was born and raised during the French occupation of the Netherlands under Napoleon. Liberation in 1813 did not automatically lead to a spiritual renewal. Rationalism, enlightenment, and easy-going civility "...continued as characteristics of the late 1700s into the new century."[2] Groen participated actively in dialogue on how the liberated nation might re-establish itself in a changing Western Europe. His most important method was writing in *Netherlandic Reflections* (*Nederlandsche Gedachten*) and *Counsel* (*Adviezen*). Today these would have been his blogs. Note the titles in the footnotes that Smitskamp consulted for these selections.

The nineteenth-century Netherlands experienced turmoil in every area of life, stirred by European revolutionary thinkers.[3] By reflection, study and action, Groen van Prinsterer discovered principles that were rooted in the Christian-historical culture of his homeland. He advocated that the gospel held as the only consistent narrative to the contemporary glib theorizing.

Dutch historian H. Algra described the movement of the gospel throughout this political and religious uprooting in his book titled *The Miracle of the Nineteenth Century*.[4] Seventy-five years of increasing flourishing in national Christian social institutions came about.

After the Nazi occupation during WWII, the nation struggled again to rebuild its institutions. A new generation meant new opportunities with assistance from the continent across the Atlantic. Smitskamp's selections from Groen's voluminous writings were timely. His foreword and the introduction by Netherlandic Prime Minister Dr. H. Colijn have been preserved in the appendix.

In another foreword, to Groen's *Unbelief and Revolution*, editor-translator Harry van Dyke wrote:

> *"Groen championed constitutional monarchy and parliamentary rights and resisted the totalitarian tendencies of liberal democracy. Although he was increasingly isolated, Groen's systematic dissent and consistent evangelical testimony resulted in the strengthening of parliamentary government and the growth of liberty."*[5]

The effects of the French Revolution were not unfamiliar to Canadian Christians before the nation was formed. Is it not a good time to collect the stories and reflect upon the principles that have shaped this young federation, Canada? What ideas have settled into the Canadian mindset? What is the "spirit of our age"? "As long as men refused to break with its spirit, the Revolution would continue to gnaw at the foundations of society."[6] Is this nation built on rock or sand? What will it take to solidify this or any nation?

Regardless of the state of material wealth and social fabric in a nation, Groen's ideas bring a fresh wind, stirring leaders of faith to robust action. More nations worldwide may benefit from such a fresh initiative.

In summary: what does Groen van Prinsterer say to us and our nation today?

Harmen Boersma
Kemptville, Ontario, Canada

A Life of Testimony and Assurance

PART I

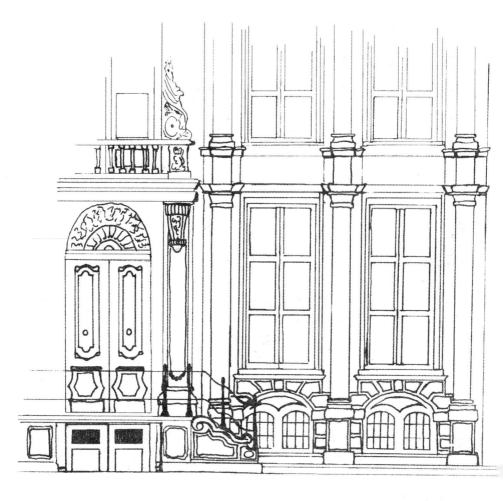

Detail of 3 Korten Vijverberg house after its restoration in the late 18th century

CHAPTER 1

Guillaume
Groen van Prinsterer

NETHERLANDIC STATESMAN,
AUGUST, 1801–MAY, 1876

Notice that aristocratic, stately designed home along the Korten Vijverberg in the centre of The Hague? So many of the buildings in that neighbourhood remind the visitor of the nation's former glory. On both sides of the front steps the narrow high windows offer an expansive view over the Hof pond. The reflecting panes brighten the sombre grey of the gable. The stark structure of the style embodies an era that has passed irretrievably. Homes are not being built like this anymore. Yet this imposing building served as a home in earlier times. On a cornerstone, passersby can read information that Groen van Prinsterer lived here for almost forty years. Like the home, so was the resident.

Groen van Prinsterer was a man of aristocratic manners, a nobleman from head to toe. By birth and relations, he belonged to the leading circles of his time. Considerable wealth allowed him to live life according to his own choosing. In addition, he was intellectually gifted, which already attracted attention when he was a student at Leiden University.

His nobility, however, was above all one of spirit and character. He never left the path that duty and calling assigned him. Selfishness and pride were completely foreign to him. His confidential correspondence, which has largely been preserved, demonstrates an exceptional purity in walk and talk. By appearance and behaviour, Groen left the impression, just like his house, of an inward, cool personality.

Superficial observers spoke of his lack of feeling and cold irony. They did not know him well! His mockery, which could cut sharply, being reserved and visibly unaffected, formed the protective armour of a tender and delicate character. The strength of his militant faith found its source in a life of intimate prayer and was constantly purified by self-examination that understood denials as a consequence of personally accepting salvation under the Lordship of Christ.

Dead orthodoxy was an abomination to him. Faith meant working responsibly in love. It was not an empty phrase, as he testified:

"When we, aware that intellectual conviction concerning the truth of the gospel has been passed onto us, yet perceive weakness and powerlessness, which grieves and discourages us, then let us, with earnest prayer, examine if the spark is missing that revives a dead and dry theology and helps it bear fruit. Faith overcomes the world! To overcome the world, it is necessary to defeat all arguments in our own heart first and all ideals that rise up against the knowledge of God and to subdue every thought into obedience to Christ."[1]

That reviving spark has been the secret of Groen's work. His poor health and long periods of illness did not prevent him from dedicating all his strength to fulfilment of his task, which he accepted as his calling. A long list of publications demonstrates his active life. They touch on all kinds of topics. They alternate between the burning issues of church and school and of state and history.

However, there is unity in this diversity. Whichever of Groen's writings one examines, they all breathe the same spirit. It is noticeable in his style of writing. They all follow the same concise and pure style. No word has been used unnecessarily. They are directed at readers who want to ponder their meaning for themselves. If one is rather satisfied with a few high-sounding slogans that are devoid of spiritual intensity, one does better not to open his texts. However, those who have taken the trouble to become familiar with Groen's manner of expression will read them with mounting interest and appreciation.

More than the style, his writings are consistent in content. Without exception, they carry forward one central thought. It is the conviction that unbelief, wherever it raises its head or in whatever form it manifests itself, always carries in it the seed of decay. Groen cannot be characterized better than a *"fighter against unbelief."*

Like a doctor who notes carefully how far a disease has spread before he starts operating, so Groen pointed out with infallible certainty how far unbelief had corroded all spheres of human society. That is why he championed the

Christian *school*, because he had concluded that unbelief had become the dominating force in education. That is why he became involved in the *church*, because he had observed that unbelief, under the name of modernism, had penetrated the church. That is why he was drawn to study *history*, because he realized that the unbelieving scholars had falsified the story of the nation. That is also why he took up the battle in *politics*, because in the political sphere he detected increasing influences of heresies rooted in unbelief.

Once his eyes had been opened, during the Belgian Revolt, to the sweeping power of the theory of unbelief, Groen decided to dedicate his life to oppose it. Initially he had little effect. The enemy he was tackling was very powerful. Among his compatriots, he hit upon halfhearted attitudes. Among his spiritual kin, he met with faintheartedness and misunderstanding. Deep disappointments were often his lot, but his energy never slackened.

What has been the result of his labour? It was more than a hundred years ago that Thorbecke, who was just starting his career at the time, reproached Groen with this remark: "You search for life among the dead; you act as a chimera; you chase after illusions that are irrevocably past."

In various ways, this accusation has been repeated since then. He is a reactionary, a bigot for medieval conditions, an obscurantist, born a few centuries too late. This is how the "educated part of the nation" labelled the opponent of revolution. Even at Groen's graveside, one of his friends testified that "Groen van Prinsterer was the last representative of an age which has passed forever."

History has clearly proven that these short-sighted statements were misplaced.

Who still makes mention of Thorbecke, not as a historical personality, who was important in his day and after, but as a leader in the troubles of *our* era? And what is left of the smug wisdom of the once dominant liberalism? However, people still inquire after and listen to Groen. Even those who opposed or disagreed with him.

Strange, don't you agree? When so much drifts, which appeared rock solid before, reflection upon the value of one's own spiritual heritage becomes a life and death question. Who decides what is worth keeping when so much is thrown overboard? Where can one find solid ground in the suction power of quicksand?

More than ever we need a guide who can show the way among the confusing mass of conflicting theories and recommended modes of behaviour.

Naturally, this reflection leads our thoughts to the past, in which our heritage was shaped and which we personally and as a nation want to preserve. Does not every generation search in history for the elements that can be useful in *their* current age? The relevance of history is always determined by contemporary needs. That relevance hits home over and again in Groen's publications.

People have rightly pointed out his weakness in not being able to leave a *concisely developed system*. However, this lack was the opposite to his virtue. Not in the practical detailed application but in sketching the big lines was his strength. Nobody has more clearly demonstrated than Groen that ultimately not popularity and force but principles are the driving power of events. Because "force can destroy people, but ideas cannot be wiped out by grape-fire." History has taught "that the uprooting of a deeply established thought system is beyond the power of the most powerful."

Every time, Groen discovered and unveiled the principles. He was gifted to do that with a blessed combination of intuition and logical analysis. He condensed an endless variety of conflicting views into a few contrasting essential principles that remain the same throughout world history. Groen especially has exposed the many forms in which unbelief revealed itself in constitutional matters by simplifying them into a limited number of repeating foundational patterns.

That is the reason why Groen's publications remain valuable. Since his death in 1876, much has changed and part of his labour has only historical value. However, every time he touches on basic questions, we can observe the similarity between then and now.

Another fact that weighed with equal importance: Groen was not only a sharp analyzer, but also a *seer*. In his home along the Korten Vijverberg, Groen outlined a wider perspective on nations than the familiar view he had overlooking the Hof pond park. He outlined cultural formation based on the principles of unbelief as they occurred in his time. In addition, he unfolded the developmental potential hidden in these principles. Especially during the last years of his life, he expressed his worry about the future—his writings took on an apocalyptic vision.

The flow of history into our times has proven that he was not wrong as far as his brushstroke descriptions are concerned. Historians in general have been described as "ruckwarts gekehrter [backwards moving, HB] prophets." Groen certainly fits that characterization.

The intent of this publication is to especially focus attention on these relevant elements in Groen's writings. Don't look for a complete picture of his teachings or his works, nor a critical treatment of his ideas concerning various topics.

We are interested in understanding his reply to the questions of *our* times; his warnings against dangers that he foresaw and predicted; and his pointers to the calling of the (Netherlandic) Christian living among these dangers.

This approach means that quotes will be plentiful. No apology for that. My task is limited to arranging his quoted ideas in a coherent presentation and with as little historical explanation as possible. *We are interested in Groen's thoughts,* not in our thoughts of Groen.

However, we don't want to completely exclude the value of his personal example. Honour and recognition, based on his position and talents, would easily have been bestowed upon him, if he had joined one of the leading political parties of his time or had been willing to make concessions. It turned out differently for him. At one time, he declared in the Second Chamber [the Netherlandic House of Commons, HB]: "To the few who are familiar with my career, my life shows all along that as often as circumstances opened up possibilities for respective appointments—I do not suggest that I could have received them—but that, in order to remain faithful to my principles, I always did that which was necessary not to receive them."[3]

Because of these principles, his whole life was an uphill struggle. His followers were almost exclusively ordinary, low-income class citizens. It was that part of the population that had no representation. He felt that in bypassing mockery and name calling, he understood, "that confessing makes one vulnerable to insults."[4] He endured them willingly, however painful they may have been. Ultimately the physical weapons are not the ones that hurt most but the spiritual ones.

Groen always found the strength to remain steadfast in that which he mentioned a few days before his death, "the only sufficient comfort in life and death which alone can resist every fiery attack, for the labourer as well as the philosopher."[5]

History demonstrates over and again how immeasurably much influence flows from a living example. In this regard, Groen has been a leader too. He is a living example of consistency of principle.

Groen van Prinsterer (Source: Picture Bank National Archives, Netherlands)

To the benefit of those who are less familiar with Groen's career, I will conclude this first chapter with a concise survey of his life.

On August 21, 1801, Guillaume Groen van Prinsterer was born in Voorburg. He was the only son of Petrus Jacobus Groen, a well-known Hague medical specialist, and Adriana Hendrika Caan, firstborn daughter of a well-to-do merchant family.

Groen's intimate memory of both his parents has been filled with thankfulness. They nurtured him with love and thoughtfulness but within the spirit and customs of that period: moderate-protestant in terms of faith and moderate-liberal in terms of his political convictions.

In 1817, the youthful Groen entered Leiden University, studying law and classical literature. Soon his giftedness attracted attention. Even before he finished in 1823 with a double degree, there was serious talk about an appointment as professor. Neither then nor later did that ever happen.

Following his academic years, Groen entered law practice, less by calling, more because he did not know himself in which direction he wanted to go. Meanwhile he intently continued studies in both fields that had attracted him from his youth: history and jurisprudence.

During this time, there are indications of a change in his views of life. The private courses of Bilderdijk, which he had taken early on, did not leave him uneffected. In general, though, he remained faithful to the views he had learned at home. Based on Groen's own admission, until about 1825 he was "Liberal and Christian; just as almost everyone else in the Reformed Christian Church (Hervormde Kerk), I was a member of the large Protestant party. Determined by the barometer of the spirit of the time, I was conservative-liberal or liberal-conservative."[6]

This period of waiting and uncertainty ended in 1827 when he somewhat unwillingly received an appointment as a referendary in the Royal Cabinet. This function, which he continued to hold until 1833 (since 1829 as cabinet secretary), was very important to the rest of his life. It put him in close contact with King Willem I and, more importantly, with the development of the events that led to the Belgian uprising. [After the liberation from France in 1813, the Netherlands consisted of the North, which was mostly Protestant, and the South, which was mixed Protestant and Catholic. The South rebelled against the government, which resulted in the new nation of Belgium. HB]

Because of his direct experiences with the practices of Revolution, a deep spiritual turnaround happened in Groen's life. In this "exceptional moment of time and at the centre of politics and polemics," he later testified, "I found my principled foundation and a clearly outlined calling, suitable to my aptitude and interests."[7]

Other circumstances and personalities have no less contributed. In Brussels, he was introduced to the Swiss pastor Merle d'Aubigne, who connected him with the Reveil. In that circle, he soon found like-minded thinkers such as Willem de Clercq and Isaac Da Costa, whose influence advanced his spiritual development.

Not the least should be acknowledged the quiet influence of his spouse, Elisabeth van der Hoop. This noble and pious Christian was his intimate life partner for almost forty years, from 1827 until his death. That their marriage was childless was the only shadow darkening their mutual happiness.

In 1833, a life-threatening illness concluded this period of spiritual conversion. In *Nederlandsche Gedachten* he wrote about it. From 1829 to 1832, it offered timely comment on the political events of the day, especially as they connected with the Belgian uprising.

Groen reappeared out of the crisis as a committed Gereformeerd Christian—and as a free man. He had offered his resignation from the king's service since his newly accepted principles conflicted ever more with the royal politics. He only retained, at his own request, supervision of the Royal House [House of Orange HB] Archives.

The next fifteen years of his life Groen spent mainly in the archives and research office. They were dedicated to advanced research of the impact of Christian principles, especially as related to constitutional law. Besides, he became increasingly absorbed in the study of Netherlandic history. In quick succession, eight exemplary volumes of the *Archives ou correspondence inedite de la maison d'Orange-Nassau* appeared. This standard work gave Groen an international reputation as historian. The documents from the private archive of the Oranges, which Groen published in part with his extensive introductions and explanations, show our history in a new and clearer light. The famous *Handbook of the History of the Fatherland,* completed in 1846, combined the results of his detailed study.

The labour on this work has been very significant in Groen's personal development. It connected him daily with his ancestors; especially with Prince Willem von Oranje, whom he deeply admired. The historical study showed him the principles that had made the Netherlands a great country. His eyes were opened to the unique culture the Reformation had revealed in the country. The understanding deepened and solidified his own conviction. He connected with the energy of the national past. In the House Archives, he became Calvinist. In addition, the study of the history sharpened his insight in the causes of Netherlandic decay.

Inevitably, the study of the eighteenth century led him into a direction that his writing in *Nederlansche Gedachten* already had taken. More expansive and equipped with greater knowledge than before, Groen explained in *Unbelief and Revolution*, published in 1847, again the causes of the political and cultural uprisings that had shaken Europe since 1789. This magnificent work, regardless of a few weak sections, became a historic-political declaration of principles that analyzed with logical arguments the revolutionary falsehoods in all its ways of branching out and in the same time pointed out a way toward restoration.

Only after 1848 did Groen become a public figure. He already had tackled contemporary issues; for example, in 1837 he made his courageous statement concerning the government action against the Afgescheidenen. [After the Reformation, the Hervormde Kerk became the state endorsed church in the Netherlands. A large group contested its changing teaching and practices and separated under the leadership of congregational pastors as the Afgescheidenen, later also named the Gereformeerden. HB] It condemned the persecution on judicial grounds. He pled for the rights of his separated faith kin. A few years later he started the polemical battle for maintaining the confession of the Hervormde Kerk.

This battle, at first against the Groninger group [named for a province in the northeast. HB], then against the increasingly popular Modernism, continued until his death. In 1840, during his brief membership in the Second Chamber, he restated his juridical principles publicly. But it was not until after the revised electoral system in 1848 that his career in parliament became possible, and consequently, political action from his perspective could commence.

With brief interludes, he sat from 1849 to 1857 and again from 1862 to 1866 in the Second Chamber.

As parliamentarian, Groen was influential, regardless of the fact that he acted almost alone. A few times he experienced strong support from a few members of the same faith, such as Mackay, Van Leyden and Elout van Soeterwoude, but he had to constantly row against a governing majority of liberals or conservatives.

He was referred to as "a marshal without an army," even though a few of his opponents recognized the truth of his statements and he found support among a not insignificant number of the Netherlandic people. However, when elections were held, his supporters could not find electoral recognition. They belonged to the "people behind the voters," who were excluded from the right to vote in the census system.

Regardless of the fact that he stood alone, Groen did not remain without influence in the Second Chamber. His knowledge and intelligence demanded attention. People knew where they stood with him. Even in this environment, he was focused on witnessing. This was based on his well-known slogan, "A statesman, no! A gospel confessor," based on his own explanation: "I don't downgrade *all* politics; I only consider *that* kind of politics as praiseworthy that is homogenous with the public conscience and with the life system that saw a nationality rise up or revive out of the battle for the Gospel...Not in juridical theories but *in the confession of the Gospel* lies my strength."[8]

For that reason, Groen always tried to lead his opponents to the principled questions. The conservatives lacked consistent action, according to Groen, and the liberals had a connection with the principles of the revolution. He frequently had principled debates with his former academic friend Thorbecke, the incarnation of liberalism. Because he considered Thorbecke his strongest opponent, Groen always tried to provoke the liberal leader.

Groen touched on many and varied topics in the chamber. His collected *Adviezen* (Counsel) display his multi-faceted involvements. But eventually he concentrated his energy on the question of education, which he considered the most urgent issue. Many times, he could justly expect success in his battle for Christian schools, but equally often it led to bitter disappointments. Bitter, because they were mostly caused by so-called kin in faith and by lack of insight and energy in his own circles.

In 1857, Van der Brugghen contributed as minister of education to a new education law that denied the rights of the Christian sector of the population. In 1866, "the most disappointing year in my grievous life time," the story repeated itself when Earl van Zuylen van Nyevelt reversed all expectations, which he could have followed based on his previous actions, for recognized Christian schools. Both times Groen felt so deeply hurt that he gave up his chamber seat.

Continuation of this parliamentary battle appeared useless to Groen:

"The cause of the repeated defeat is the indifference and superficiality, year after year, of the majority of the allies of faith in leading circles, even among church ministers, whose calling seemed essential in defending the interests of the Christian population, for freedom of conscience for the Christian in society...The story of my own life and that of the party of which I was the leader can be summarized concisely in two phrases. My friends have finally defeated me at our own game. A party that undermines its leader loses much of its strength."[9]

Following his last disappointment, Groen could no longer be persuaded to run for a seat again. He did assist in rebuilding anti-revolutionary party representation in parliament. In the election of 1871, he resolutely broke cooperation with all half-hearted friends by recognizing only three candidates for his party, namely the trio Kuyper, Keuchenius and Van Otterloo. This breakaway from many with whom he had had a long-lasting friendship was difficult. However, it was a freeing decision for him. The regained independence for his party provided new energy.

Outside of parliament, Groen was also very active. For five years, from 1850 to 1855, he almost singlehandedly edited his daily *De Nederlander*, until it became too much for him. It did not bring about a following. Even after he had withdrawn for good from the chamber, he continued to contribute to irregularly published issues of *Parliamentary Studies and Sketches,* with his descriptive and editorial articles highlighting the current events locally and internationally. The second series of *Nederlansche Gedachten* commenced in 1869 and basically continued this labour of interest.

In addition, he continued to develop his organizational activities. Electoral associations that turned to him for advice about candidates could count on his full cooperation. The establishment of the Society for Christian-National Schools, which contributed so much to the battle for Christian schools, owed its existence to Groen's initiative, and for years he was its sole leader.

All along, he produced a continuous stream of documents touching on the urgent issues in church and school, state and history, all with the same purpose: to enlighten his kin of faith and to challenge them to action.

Only after he approached seventy did Groen slowly withdraw himself from the daily battle. In Dr. Abraham Kuyper, he welcomed a successor who could take over his labour and whose voice, more than Groen's, penetrated the kleine luyden (common folk) who formed the basis of his support. This succession meant much to him. Groen understood that he lacked the gift of popular speech. He was convinced that "The orthodox people (mostly because of the fear of God yet unreached by the continually expanding influence of unbelief) have never been unfaithful while I was faithful."[10] This faithfulness was more based on intuitive support than understanding of his ideas.

Groen's *emeritaat*, as he referred to his retirement, did not lead to idleness. In the latter copies of the *Nederlandsche Gedachten* and in other later documents, he returned to the love of his youth: history. These writings became more autobiographical in nature. Even in the descriptions of the experiences of his own life, Groen did not belie his own nature; continually he returned to emphasize the principles for which he had spent his energy.

To the end of his life, his mind remained clear, even though his health continued to deteriorate. After a short illness, he died peacefully on May 19, 1876. This robust fighter entered the eternal rest.

CHAPTER 2

Groen's Apocalyptic Vision

G roen did not endure the struggle of his life's work because he found encouragement in the success of it. On the contrary, he experienced disappointment after disappointment. He did not overly value immediate results, but they would have been joyfully accepted. The faithful don't hurry. He witnessed:

"Even during the grief of continual disappointments, I am not convinced that my work is a useless and ridiculous struggle against the spirit of the century. One could equally mock the farmer, I said in the Second Chamber, who continually throws the seed on his field without practical gain other than the dying of the seed. Its development and fruit does not depend on the immediately intended result, which perhaps will appear in another era and under other circumstances. That is how it is supposed to be. Season and time is only known by the Lord. Our ways are not His ways; but truth remains truth so it can *ultimately* find acceptance in every God-fearing heart."[1]

This conviction formed the basis of Groen's hope for the future. He observed an increasing aversion to God and His Word in the Netherlands. Consequently, he foresaw sooner or later a national decay and debasement. This increase in pressure could be beneficial to the strengthening of true principles. "The tribulation of the homeland [can] be a means to convict at least a few that the flourishing of the nations cannot be found in their policy unless the will of the revealed God is accepted as its foundation for justice and devotion to duty and responsibility."[2]

Experience is a good teacher. "The nation will not lack an understanding of the anti-revolutionary ideas when it realizes that the revolutionary wisdom shows enmity to all that was appreciated in this land by its religious and free ancestors."[3]

Although Groen's era offered few hopeful signs, he did not exclude a better future for the Netherlands. He obtained this optimism from its history. When in 1831, because of French support for the Belgian mutineers, the Netherlands found itself in a perilous situation, Groen called out to his countrymen: "Keep courage! A nation perishes when it loses its character; during the fifteen years of miserable unity, there was more reason to fear the extinction of the Netherlands than now."

"In 1572, Prince Willem I ruled only a small section of Holland and out of it grew the commonwealth of shires (het Gemeenebest). How did that come about? By God's grace, by courage and endurance that was founded on solid principles. Let us model the endurance of our ancestors. When the worst happens, the Netherlandic people will not only demand respect in their fall, but perhaps offer a long series of experiences that demand respect in their rebirth and restoration."[4]

Therefore "discouragement does not behoove the *Netherlander* nor the *Christian*. When persuasion seems impossible, witnessing remains a duty. He may be powerless, just as Prince Willem I stood alone in the eyes of the world yet counted on the almighty Ally, who raises people up in His own time. He will be known for the ultimate triumph of his chosen principles, regardless of the cheers of his adversaries. We can learn from our national history that an era of complete despondency often has been a period of preparation for blessed outcomes."[5]

Pressure put on a nation may not be its greatest disaster. Loss of national independence, a wonderful privilege, is not the greatest doom that can hit. "Even during the worst humiliation or enslavement there can be a blessing and a preparation for a better future. Over Jena, [an old town on the Saale river in Thuringia, East Germany. This is a reference to the battle of Jena in 1806 in which Napoleon defeated a Prussian army. HB] and along a route of national humiliation under God's leading lay the way for a deeply fallen Prussia to unknown prosperity.

"The worst is (and may God's mercy protect the Netherlands from it) when a nation, which in world history has been known to live under God's blessings, according to the testimony of the Gospel, through its own denervation becomes bastardized—when a nation commits national suicide of its soul and forfeits its right to live already before its death sentence."[6]

Groen's favourable apocalypse contained a reservation. Restoration remains an option but lasting results can only be delivered when it is sought in the one true direction:

"The guarantees for the future of the Netherlands lie in holding onto the Netherlandic principles. In their religious expression, the people have not completely lost these—Thank God!—in the sense of liberty which we inherited from our ancestors.

"Lasting recovery is only possible when there is a blessing on the preaching of the Word. It can expose any worldly wisdom. The Netherlands could take the test of the undeceiving promise: 'Seek first the kingdom of God and His righteousness, and all these things will be added unto you.' (Matthew 6:33).

"If, in a Christian sense, the Netherlands desired to be a devout and salvation loving country, it would be counted among the nations that trust the far reach of God's promises. Blessed Netherlands...if it felt the need to return to the God whose favour, often forfeited, perhaps is still waiting. Maybe it will learn that every revision of the constitution begins with the acceptance of God's law. By confessing and worshiping, it once more could have the foresight to become a paragon of God's grace for many generations."[7]

Following these rather optimistic sounding remarks, we recognize among Groen's views also those with a sombre tone. The future can bring redemption and restoration, but another option is still possible, although there is no certainty about that now.

"The future," as stated in the epilogue of Groen's story of the homeland history, "is more than ever hidden in dark clouds. The same apostasies keep branching out in church, state and all of society. People will gather what they have sown. What will the fortunes of the Netherlands be? Will it be dissolved into the larger nations, or is hope justified that the seemingly dead ways can be revived and healed with new energy? It is uncertain!

"But what is certain is that the history of the Netherlands, blessed in the past century with excellent privileges, still witnesses the infallible promises and the curses of God. The future will still reveal the distinction between the righteous and the godless; between those who serve Him and those who do not. Every exchange of punishment and blessing becomes a reason to describe the continuation of this page of human history with a tone of thankfulness and worship."[8]

During his lifetime, Groen observed continual indications in events and opinions that filled him with fear for growing decay and the far-reaching dominance of heresy. He remained hopeful for redemption under God's blessing following a return to Him. "However, that hope was thwarted as Europe and the Netherlands insisted on ignoring the lessons of experience and the voice of Providence. Both would need to feel still more the yoke of the Almighty. It had become obvious during a half century of lament, when their policies did not recognize a guide outside of human invention and only caused the interchange of unrest and arbitrary decisions. God does not bless godless theories nor concepts by which He is not honoured. They are a deceitful foundation of state regulations, ruling families and the happiness of nations."[9]

As the revolution theory gained ground, the future perspective became more sombre. Especially since these theories "from an unbelieving point of view are indisputable. They are the kind that invoke fanaticism so much more easily because they are being inflamed by hope of satisfying passions and lusts. They reveal a reason for anxiety that is caused by possible, potential, unavoidable new outbursts. We discover that the realization of these godless ideals clash with impassable obstacles in the general nature of things themselves. We become aware that the renewal of proof, already loaded for double impact and on a far wider scale, could lead to any kind of reign of terror and despotism. Fear does not seem to be unreasonable for scenes of confusion, looting and murder with tragic results that will make the French Revolution look like a lovely picnic."[16]

Groen spoke these words in 1846. Much of what he feared became reality later. Already in 1848, a new wave of revolution had flamed up in Paris that threatened all of Europe. The Netherlands too was in danger of being affected by it.

Based on these events, Groen wrote in that same year: "There are nights when one can see ahead merely a hand's length. We experience such a night in politics. Conjecturing and guessing is allowed, and everyone seems to take advantage of it. However, more can be done than only conjecturing and guessing in relation to these happenings and their consequences in general.

"False theories surely cannot do more than cause calamity and decay. One can be sure that popular government really ends up revealing the arbitrariness of those who roused, flattered and cheated the people to serve their own desire for leadership, profiteering or lust for revolutionary experiments. It is for certain that the lawlessness that now appears in violence caused by radicals and communists or reactionaries and conservatives will end. But which of these alternatives has the best chance? How and when can out of this uproar come a situation of regularity and order?"[10]

Groen put forward various possibilities, but all of them were equally alarming. After 1848, when the "might makes right" attitude and national egotism became more openly evident in European society, the number of hopeful possibilities increased rather than decreased.

It is no surprise that Groen's pronouncements became increasingly more apocalyptic. Every time the days grow dark, the expectation of the end of times is revived in the Christian's mood. Under pressure and distress, faith in the future promise of God becomes real. Groen saw the era of his lifetime as a period of preparation and change. His reflection in the light of Revelation, of the signs of the times, brought him to the conclusion that "the agitation of all kinds of theories and the turmoil of conflicting dispositions shows the approaching battle between light and darkness, which world history has yet to feel in extent and grimness."

That future is not foreign to the gospel believer. "The heavenly light not only fulfills divine judgments in the events of the past, it also shines (just as lightning rips through the clouds) on the dark paths of the future toward us as if out of the mystery of higher spheres. We know the *prophecies:* increase of decay, general spread of a lapse, increase in temptations, public appearance of the false angel of light, general oppression of those faithful to the Lord, fear of the future."[11]

But more was predicted. Therefore "among all uncertainty, the Christian can be certain: feel safe in times of danger, experience peace during unrest, see light even in dark days. We walk by faith, not by sight. In faith, there is a future: the return of Him who promised to reappear as He had gone up to heaven.

"When? When the Good News of the Kingdom has been preached through-out the world as a witness to all nations. When false prophets arise and lead many astray. When unrighteousness increases and the love of many grows cold. When tribulation appears to such a scale as has not happened since the beginning of the world. When there will be wars and rumours of wars, extensive earthquakes, famine and pestilence. When the nations will be full of fear and doubt. When the sea and its waves will roar and people's confidence will fail for fear of the things that might still happen on the earth. When the Antichrist will appear, rul-ing under Satan's influence, filled with power, signs and wonders of the lie. Only then will the Son of Man appear on a cloud with great power and glory. When God will be pleased to reveal the times and the moments only He has determined" (Matthew 24:3-44; 2 Thessalonians 1:3-2:17).[12]

Whether this future is near or far away, we don't know. It is better not to guess and to calculate "because the shortsighted mortal is not allowed vainly to run ahead of God's judgments and to lift the veil with which He covers the mysteries of world government."[13]

We do know that the leading of world government is determined by Him. It helps to see things in the proper perspective, which determines the measure of their importance. "Christ is the beginning and the end in the annals of humanity. Holy Scripture lays out God's plan. The efforts and intentions of minute humans in each era (which may seem valid and important in their eyes) only compare as side issues in the design of the Eternal, the Lord of heaven and earth. They can only be as valid as they tie in with the main plan.

"God's plan is clearly recorded in the Bible. In Genesis, victory of the rule of Christ over the deceiver of humanity was revealed already (Genesis 3:15; Revelation 18-22). Redemption is sure for those who are grafted into the Saviour by a true faith. Everything that occurs is subjected to the fulfillment of this plan."[14]

Regardless of the darkness ahead, this conviction offers peace and courage. "Among turmoil, inflamed by human wisdom and human passions, we are founded in Him, who according to the steadfast Word of prophecy, leads the development of the fate of the world to a certain and glorious end. Christ Himself will raise the banner and destroy the exorbitant pride with the breath of His mouth. [It is] the heart and conclusion of history, the history of the future and of eternity. Its source of knowledge is the Word of God, its assurance lies in God's faithfulness, its glory shines in God's love, its actual settlement will be in the glorious or catastrophic experience on the other side of the grave."[15]

National Leaders Follow Principles

Follow

Principles

PART II

CHAPTER 3
What Is The Revolution?

"Then came the French Revolution which...broadcast in the world those pernicious principles from which it still suffers and will continue to suffer until it has repudiated them. It proclaimed the rights of men to the contempt of the rights of God" (Emile Legal).*

O ne of Groen van Prinsterer's most well-known works has the title *Unbelief and Revolution*. This title also states his program. It describes an idea that guided him through all his political actions. He highlighted this idea continually from all angles. He discovered an unbreakable and irrevocable connection between unbelief and Revolution. Groen's understanding of unbelief does not need an extensive explanation. It is the rejection of God's revealed truth.

To understand Groen's train of thought, one needs to know his style of speech. Being unfamiliar with it has many times led to making caricatures of his ideas. When we talk about revolution, we usually mean the placing of sovereignty in the state, or at least an attempt to place it there. Groen does use that meaning at times. It is not the reason why he called himself "anti-revolutionary." Less well-known is his meaning of the term "Revolution."

---

* Emile Legal, a French Oblate missionary who worked in Ontario and Western Canada alongside Father Lacombe; from the introduction to his *Short Sketches of the History of the Catholic Churches and Missions in Central Alberta*, Winnipeg: West Canada Publishing Co., 1914, p. 7. Quoted in *Legacy: How French Canadians Shaped North America*, edited by Andre Pratte and Jonathan Kay. Toronto: McClelland & Stewart, 2016.

Political changes such as the one in the Netherlands in the sixteenth century and the one in England in 1688 [elsewhere referred to as the Glorious Revolution, HB] received his full approval. He labeled them "conservative, Christian-historical, exceptionally anti-revolutionary" revolutions, which differed cosmically from the "revolutionary" revolution.[1]

When Groen chose the name "anti-revolutionary party" for his political party, he meant not just to express opposition to the French Revolution of the 1790s. This misconception was the reason people accused him repeatedly of fighting hoaxes. It would indeed be a waste of effort to defend oneself against a political event that as a historical event cannot be undone.

No! When Groen mentions *the* Revolution, he does not refer to one specific event in the past but rather to a permanent attitude, of which the French revolution was a most important occurrence. However, it was only one manifestation!

The Revolution means rather, "the systematic turnover of ideas by which the laws of God are replaced with human arbitrary wisdom and decisions as the foundation of rights and truth for the State and Society."[2] Out of this Revolution, which for the first time was revealed in the French Revolution and which continued afterwards to express itself in European State formations, came "all its various theoretic and practical ways and forms that resulted from the application and development of unbelief."[3]

Groen extensively explained this development in *Unbelief and Revolution*. First, he highlighted the false ideas people believe were the cause of *The* Revolution. Then he discussed the principles out of which *The* Revolution flowed. To the former, he counted especially the Reformation and existing abuses. Even in Groen's time, adherents of the Church of Rome and nominal Protestants blamed the Reformation. He observed a completely opposite reason.

Then he described the principles that he believed caused revolution. He took an opposite position when he stated, "The Revolution, in relation to world history, has been the opposite of the Reformation to Christianity. The Reformation saved Europe from idolatry, but revolution brought civilization to the abyss of unbelief. Equal to Reformation, Revolution penetrates every area of human practice and scholarship. In the former, obedience to God, while in the latter, rebellion to God is the foundational idea."

Elsewhere he summarized that contrast like this: "Revolution grew out of the sovereignty of humans, Reformation the sovereignty of God. The first judges revelation by means of reason, while the other subjects reason to revelation. The former uproots individual views, the latter unifies them in faith. Revolution frazzles social and family ties, Reformation bundles and blesses them. The first maintains ground by murdering and killing, while the other overcomes with martyrs. The former arises out of the abyss, while the latter descends out of heaven."[4]

Groen acknowledged that the principles of the Reformation after their first explosive development tended to diminish. People looked for other ways to stem the stealthy abuses under the "ancient rêgime." After all excesses had been put aside, there could be "enough evidence of dissatisfaction with the direction of government and blurring of the formation of the state. People rightly desired far-reaching reforms under the pretence of their sense of justice and humanity." But Groen resisted explaining Revolution by those feelings.

The supporters of Revolution early on were very one-sided and unreasonable in their critique of the past. "In their summary of past corruptions, they kept silent about everything that softened and justified them. Always the wrong was highlighted, never the good. Scenes were created for which images and illustrations were taken only from injustices, corruptions and shamefulness."[5]

Secondly, the corruptions were not serious enough to declare a revolution such as the one in France. These abuses were merely "minor causes of the Revolution...The degeneration of European states was enough reason to cause a terrorizing outburst, since reforming wisdom was lacking."

"But a changeover is not *the* Revolution. To cause this systematic revolt against social structures and comfortable life, to create *this kind of* Revolution, took more than portraying the worst and numerous abuses. A change that demonstrates in every aspect signs of a theoretical development must have theoretical origins."[6]

Research into the theoretical roots of Revolution led Groen to the views that became prominent in Europe in the eighteenth century. People were searching rightly for improvement and did so with diligence and vigour. However, "energy wrongly directed becomes more condemning as it becomes more powerful: the beauty of a mountain stream does not reduce its icy impact, as the destructive flash flood covers the land below. There was an abundance of fireworks and torchlights, but sunlight was absent. No human wisdom will make a field fruitful without the light of the sun. The results of the human mind and genius are useless in producing thought patterns and forming social systems when they are purposely done without considering divine inspiration and deny the difference of freedom and independence explored in philosophy."[7]

People emancipated themselves from faith in the revealed truth and searched for their foundation in humankind. "The origin of this philosophy was the *sovereignty of Reason*, which led to materialism and renouncing God. Supremacy of reason was put forward as an axiom. When reason is considered infallible, revelation cannot trump it with transcending arguments. Reason became the norm for truth."

Consequently, one deception was inevitably followed by others. "When reason is elevated to the top, revelation soon defaults into a collection of legends and fables; nature is being explained out of natural processes when one is blinded to revelation; religion becomes mere abstraction, an image, an imaginary deity. To maintain belief, people have to understand something not understandable and less believable than God."[8]

This kind of unbelief already reigned in ancient times. But in the eighteenth century it became dominant in European society. The exception became the rule. Even among heathen nations, people generally held onto the notion of divine revelation. In the age of enlightenment, humankind entertained the discovery "that people are their own lawgivers, every revelation is a deception. God Almighty, the Creator of heaven and earth, is an absurdity, or at least superfluous."[9]

Even those who clothed this unbelief in the more attractive form of deism and claimed identity as Christian ultimately based it on the denial of the basic principles of the Christian faith. People referred to "the Upper Being, rather than the Living God who reveals Himself in His Word; to decorative terms as Christendom and Christian slogans because the essential gospel disappears as soon as a personal Saviour is relegated to the background."

In every sphere of society, this unbelief infiltrated people's minds and mood. It caused "a worldwide crisis, including a crisis in the history of the Christian church: a period of decline and decay and open resistance to the gospel in the spheres of scholarship and practice."[10] It also touched the areas of constitutional law and politics.

There exist quite a large number and variety of constitutional systems. At one end of the spectrum are the debaucheries of permanent revolution and anarchy and at the other end the established order of supreme state authority, with many variations in between. However, the demarcation line between them "does not depend on the outer form of the systems. When all is traced back to their ground motif, there are in fact only two systems of a fundamental nature. Systems that in appearance look different sometimes are essentially closely related. What really matters is that in dealing with all of constitutional law between two options only one choice needs to be made. There is essentially only one contrast at stake in the political battle of our century. In all countries, eras and forms of government, the nature and essence, the origin and character of the highest power is the issue: *is sovereignty from humankind or is it from God?*"11

Revolutionary thought—this reveals its origin in unbelief—rejects the sovereignty of God. From this one error, all others follow. Instead of the revealed justice of God, they preach the statutes of mankind—especially their right to freedom.

First, reason is declared sovereign and autonomous. Then "freedom of thought and action. Supremacy of the *mind* and the *will* of humans. Infallibility of speech and the heart follows. Humans by their nature are good: what is the origin of evil then? If humans are inclined to do good and show love for neighbour, why is it that there exists so much anxiety in society for criminality and human passion?

"The revolutionary philosophy finds the answers in the systems: because of bad systems the original goodness in human nature has been misdirected. The inclinations and passions present in human nature have been moved into an opposite direction. Therefore, all that is needed is a change in the systems, the removal of anything that blocks freedom and humans can follow their inclinations and passions, the means to rebuild and perfect the state."

An authority that is not sanctioned by people does not fit in this theory. "Dismantling of independence from any authority is from an unbeliever's point of view taking away humiliating abuse. It is certainly fitting in this view since unbelief only understands *human* authority. The denial of *droit divin* is the 'source' of liberalism and of the enthusiasm it arouses. The liberal theory is connected to the elevation of human nature. Humans are too great to bow to neighbours when they give commands in their own name."12

However, somehow authority needs to be established. "There is a society and a state. There should be a society and a state if we do not desire barbarity. Authority, rights, duties and inequality are a given. When the historic state is dissolved—listen up!—how is the revolutionary state formed?"

Groen's answer: "How is the state formed? How to legally bind free and equal people? By voluntary agreements only. If the revolutionary understanding of freedom and equality is the foundation of one's structure, authority and right are conventional. If the state is to develop without terror, then its origin can only be that of social contract."13

This is how the system of revolutionary popular sovereignty came into existence. The government holds the mandate of the sovereign people, executor of the popular will on which its authority is based. Eighteenth-century philosophers declared that this system would provide heaven on earth.

"Implementation of these philosophical guidelines would delineate prejudice and tyranny, establish freedom, guarantee welfare, affluence, civilization and great pleasure in life. This utopia would lead to the recreation and perfection of humanity. Jealousy and disagreements would be eliminated; the happiness of each person would fall in line with the happiness of everyone. There would be peace on earth. Truth, justice, mutual love and obedience would come out of natural guidelines. Rather than binding them, satisfying of desires and passions, mutual support and brotherhood would follow; rather than misery, bliss would occur. What had not been possible in times of ignorance could finally happen."[14]

This was the argument of the revolutionary idealists. But their hope was a whim. Even when we wait with the question, what happened with the theory in practice, we can already figure out where it had to lead. Eventually there is no other choice than between anarchy or dictatorship. The system of popular will can be implemented in these two ways and has been set up in either of them. Either the sovereign people reserve the power for themselves which cripples government when it acts differently, or the people delegate their sovereignty to the government which then receives the free decision power over the life and property of its subjects.

What is the consequence of the first choice? It appears that everyone who has adopted the irresistible popular will as a guideline for all governments out of necessity recognizes a kind of forgiving, dutiful or, in revolutionary terms, a holy rebellion. The excellence of the purpose offers significant freedom in the choice of the means.

Groen's contemporary, bright Christian philosopher Julius Stahl, has offered a concise fair judgment about this reign according to the popular will. "Such a type of government," he writes, "cannot exist because of the nature of its foundational principle. The king has no power in balance with parliament, and based on the same principle, parliament has no power in balance with the masses. Indeed, the law itself is subjected to it since it is its own creation. The people's fickleness, when elevated to sovereign power, causes a continual revolution."[15]

The second choice is equally unattractive. "There is freedom and equality, a social contract, a *state* for which unity rests on the sovereignty of the popular will. How is that will formed and activated? From the bottom up, by means of the right to vote, the popular authority is centrally embodied. From there it provides, as sovereign state authority representing the people, to the people the law, while suppressing all resistance. There are no limits to this type of authority, nor can it ever be secondary. Thus, the state is almighty, meddlesome and the sole ruler. Its only guideline is the interest of the state. It demands that 'the dearest and highest goods' (named in various ways, for example, general well-being, national happiness) be sacrificed to the interest of the state."

It is of little importance in which form this revolutionary state presents itself. It can be republican. Nothing hinders "the popular sovereignty with its misery of disarray and oppression. It operates where a single person or a monarchical family reigns." In the latter instance, it is, as Groen labels it, "the single-head popular sovereignty, the popular will concentrated in one person."[16]

"But you ask, how is it possible that such a single theory that sprouts such arbitrary options can be declared a theory of freedom? What guarantees does this supremacy, which is elevated higher than anything referred to as God, offer that it does not turn to abuse and oppression? What guarantees?"

"Every apologist of the revolution theory will argue that the whole system rests on guarantees. Just notice the popular origins of all powers. It is the totality of citizens from whom the popular will flows. They have a right to state protection even as they reign themselves. Their freedom and autonomy is the source of the state. Its approval is the highest law. Anyone who has been trusted with some power and who abuses it at the expense of the popular sovereignty is being checked by the freedom to hold elections, use the press and divert popular opinions. If necessary, such views may be suppressed and punished."[17]

This is the theory! In a next chapter, we will see how these ideals are being worked out in practice, but even without considering the practice, this theory clearly, because of its principles, cannot be acceptable to the Christian. The revolution theory is *anti-Christian*. It places evil into the systems and puts all expectations of good in humans.

This theory poses that "mankind is naturally good. Their inborn excellence has become unrecognizable because of superstition and suppression. When breaking these ties, perfection of the state will happen quickly. Christians understand that humans are prone to do evil; we know that systems are designed by mankind, not mankind designed by systems. Every state rule causes either benefits or disaster, depending upon the principles that give it life.

"When we summarize the complete idea behind the system and consider the happiness that may be expected in an immense future utopia, let us compare it with the unrelenting revealed truth. Can we honestly doubt that enmity between the seed of the woman and the seed of Satan in the sphere of state is avoidable? In a real revolutionary state, can tolerance be expected for the living gospel? Just to resist God, just to ignore Him, just to be as God and to replace God with oneself, just to destroy God if possible, humans arrive at the bottom of systemic godlessness, and it makes them equal to their own system."[18]

Even though most followers of this philosophy and its consequences have second thoughts about sticking with it and they find it hard to accept the conclusions, the correctness of the conclusions is not diminished. Besides being anti-Christian, the revolutionary philosophy is also *anti-historical*.

Certainly, her followers have often enough based their claims on history. "Apparently not without proof. The superfluous ways of treating history was advantageous to followers who sought enough examples that appeared supportive of their loose principles. The torch of the newly proposed wisdom was eagerly applied to interpret all of history. It led them into the most fruitful source of historical error, according to Montesquieu (regardless of him falling into it regularly too), and applied their own imaginations to people and ages that were once foreign to them. Just like dreams carry on that which has kept the mind busy throughout the daytime, it is not surprising that the learned memory of the revolutionaries is reciprocated in the visions they presented as historical truth. History became a false witness that acted as a powerful tool to steer public opinion into the direction of the revolutionary thought. History became a museum full of revolutionary samples and an arsenal of revolutionary tools to suppress the truth."[19]

Since this claim to history is an essential characteristic of every revolution that rises out of this theory, it breaks with the past. That too is the result of its principles. It pretends to have the only true solution for every difficulty. Before revolution came along, everything was evil. It must be cleared out of the way. "Whoever embraces these theories, opposing the essence of every state, can certainly not by removal of former traditions be satisfied. Rather he will feel called to destroy all that the wisdom of ancestors and the flow of the ages have established...Demolishing is unavoidable sometimes when it involves not renovation but building up from a completely new foundation. Hesitation did not fit with demolishing of that which, as they argued, brought steady damage to the rights of humans and citizens. The revolutionary liberation could not allow any obstacles in the way of its glorious endeavours. The ripping up of the social fabric of obtained rights, woven throughout societal entities, was done without a qualm. The true life of the nation would commence only with signing onto the new political form."[20]

This describes the expectation of the theory. How was the practice?

CHAPTER 4

The Revolution Theory in Practice

O ne of Groen's basic ways of interpreting history is identifying the chain of events that happens mostly as the result of principles at work. Once a vision has become a people's mindset, the application will follow undoubtedly in practice.

The revolutionary theory demonstrates that process. For *Unbelief and Revolution,* Groen spent much research on the way in which the theory has been realized. He particularly demonstrated this in the development of the French Revolution. But he also identified clearly the influence of the revolutionary theories including his own lifetime. My [Dr. H. Smitskamp's, HB] intention here is not to follow his [Groen's, HB] documentation point by point. I rather show the general themes, which always and everywhere mark the application of the theory.

First note this peculiarity: the revolutionary theory strives for perfect and consequential realization. When one is convinced that "redemption" can only be expected from the general application of the principles that one favours, every effort will be made to bring them into practice.

Therefore, during the early period of every revolution, the most stringent party will get the upper hand. Those less convinced, those who doubt the consequences of their theory and want to put the brakes on, are being trampled. Compared to the fanatic followers, the doubters are always wrong.

Consider, for example, development that led to the reign of terror in 1793-94 during the French Revolution. How can it be explained that Robespierre and

51

his small cohort could force their will upon the French people? "Faithfulness to his own convictions, even if he was left by himself, could not hold him back from the last and worst consequences. A selflessness focused only on the triumph of the theory. It gave him a natural ascendency over others who doubted and tried to halt the terrorism that they approved in principle. Only the conviction gave him the drive, in word and deed, to ascend over those who *doubted*, just because they *doubted*."

Robespierre and his followers "dedicated their life to a worldview they believed not only true, good, beneficial and salutary, but the only and unquestionable means to start uninterruptable happiness everywhere that would end catastrophe and evil soon. When we place ourselves in the mood in which they imagine having received the apostolate of such a 'gospel,' only then can we form an understanding how the force of confessors who, fanned by the content of the confession, heightened their passion or rather their fanaticism. We should not judge this fanaticism as extreme. Rather it was free of excitement; it was supported by reasoning of the mind rather than the intoxication of passions. It was the submission to a theory by which deceptive world re-creation was accepted without doubt. Consequently, they responded to an awareness of a higher, self-assuring calling in their acts of violence. It created the cold-blooded, relentless energy of the revolutionaries."[1]

Was this attitude exaggerated? Those who support the revolution theory but not the violence would like us to think so. Unjustifiably so! "Not the will of the people but the force of the principles has triumphed. People, regardless of their flattering that they can be masters of the principles, are dragged along against their will and choice. 1793 arrived not because the revolutionaries had it predicted or wished, rather it followed the development of the theory that triumphed in 1789. There is no exaggeration but application. It followed a marked path accomplished by sidelining humaneness along the way."

The consequentists were in the right. "With their claim to the noblest principles, endorsing the well-being of the state and maintaining the revolution, which caused the overthrow of the faithless or doubting government, every apparent irregularity was allowed. It became a duty and was greeted with praise." Even about the choice of means, "every accusation is unfair and unfitting. There is no other measurable limit than the measure of a subjective urge. It therefore comes down to convenience, which is a subjective emotion. As a question of conscience, note that the mind and the heart cannot answer otherwise; either the personal conviction, which no other than the criminal knows, that his perceived deed was necessary or useful in the interest of the changeover of the state."

"Although the revolutionaries generally hold enmity against the Jesuits, there is no worse and more complete Jesuitism than that which develops out of the revolutionary theory. The accusation, the justification, the sanctification of every means lies in *the wellbeing of the state*: wherever this becomes the drive and the guide, injustice becomes just. Out of a sense of duty to their idol, people sacrifice truth, fairness and humaneness. This explains the cold-bloodedness with which the worst misdeeds have been performed: the solidity of conviction and the enthusiasm with which the aggressive party pronounced their sentence for destruction of everything that stood in its way."[2]

Surprisingly, the rule of terror, regardless of being driven by the revolutionaries, was rather short. It did not establish that which it considered consequent with its theory. That should not be surprising, since it matches the nature of revolution. Here shows its secondary characteristic: it *never* gets completely realized. The reason is that the revolutionary theories clash with the creation order of God and therefore with the reality of history and the essence of human nature. They can never freely and completely develop. "Instead, exposed by nature and history, they continually run into trouble that increasingly gets more difficult to overcome and finally is unconquerable.

"The sun shines equally clear for all, even though the blind cannot see it. Denying unchangeable laws cannot raise the lie to the truth. Denying God does not mean destroying Him. Perfection of human nature does not follow the denial of human decay. We may declare as error and prejudice the historical development of nations, the created origin of justice and authority, the supremacy of God even over earthly gods and governments, the relation between church and state, each with their mutual independence and responsibilities. These are and remain pillars in public justice. No wonder the revolution theory remains constantly embattled by human conscience, the true human needs, the nature of the state in its various forms and the obtained rights and freedoms."[3]

Revolution is very capable of breaking down but not able to build up. This shows the second characteristic: revolution has never been able to provide what it promised. Especially the promise of freedom in the civil sphere was never accomplished. Why? "All freedoms have been made dependent on a false image of freedom because they are not agreeable with the maintenance of lawful authority and the holiness of the state. People seek their security in an order that reveals itself in the destruction, not the protection of freedoms.

"When people want freedom, it is important that they connect with true freedom. It is not found in systemic licentiousness, but in submission to the laws that inseparably advance flourishing of state and society. The freedom that is submissive to the perceived equality and popular sovereignty is a force that brings disorder and destruction."4

The same happened to the other ideals the revolution pursued, such as justice and tolerance, humaneness and morality. How did they turn out? These valuable attributes became opposite in practice because their source was purposely hidden. These fruits cannot be grown in the revolutionary field, "only developed in a Christian environment. Only in the gospel can they truly be found.

"The ancient, classic cultures had only a weak reflection of them. Through the preaching of the gospel did they become popular, still unknown to the pagan world. This rich inheritance has fallen into the lap of philosophy, rather than treasured by orthodoxy.

"How have they been treated? Regardless of her assurance, these treasures have been lost in her care. No wonder! Philosophers liked the fruits but rejected the Christian principles. How can one enjoy cool waters after the source has been blocked? Or enjoy the shade of trees after the roots have been cut? Their calculation has always become miscalculation. The trees along the banks of the gospel stream, fruitfully in blossom when replanted to a dry land without stream, withered. Admittedly, there is silliness and incompleteness in the comparison.

"In the poisonous field of idolatry, they became disastrous crops whose deadly venom is hidden in glorious colours and lovely perfumes. Magic words that supposedly called for perfection of wisdom and happiness remained constantly blasted empty sounds. The results were the opposite to the imaging: justice turned into injustice, freedom turned into force, tolerance became persecution, humanity became inhumanity and morality became immorality."5

The third characteristic may now be observed: reaction. It should not be surprising that revolution, when not delivering what it promised after a period of breakdown and licentiousness, unavoidably brought forward a reaction: "The glory of the movement does not last forever; the current, which ran over all barriers, comes to a halt. Every step that seems to bring the enthusiastic zealot closer to his goal shows the more innocent onlooker the impossibility of reaching it.

The theory continually tightens its demands until the futile triumph is over-stretched and it explodes under the growing opposition. How long a systematic error can move on is uncertain."

"However, it is certain that the revolution will come to a halt. The expectation of an unconditional application will pass sometime by revealing itself simply in bitter complaining. A minority may through fanaticism and physical force be able to keep the upper hand for a while. The time will come in which forceful action is impossible and the force of destruction gives way to the cry for survival."6 Ultimately people could not survive in an environment of anarchy. They longed for a strong leader who somehow could turn chaos into order. [*Compare with the stories in the Old Testament book of Judges. HB*]

Groen considered the restoration of an ordered society a privilege. Considering the containment of revolutionary stirrings that upset France in 1848, he wrote: "I really don't regret that in 1849 the reaction triumphed over pure radicalism. I not only appreciate the talents that bridled it, but for the system itself I have conditional praise. In some circumstances, because of the revolutionary terror, reactionary force may be needed and required. A necessary evil that slows down a worse evil can prove to be a blessing of immeasurable value. Then I am thankful for such a blessing and don't think that it proves me unfaithful to my original principles."

"Often I have said, the reactionary is a revolutionary, who contradicts his own theory. I repeat again! Does it follow that I always reject resistance? No! Persistence is praiseworthy, as long as one persists in that which is good...No, I don't pronounce an unconditional sentence on systematic efforts of reversal. I understand that the execution of September laws is sometimes unavoidable." (The so-called September laws, directed at revolutionary movements and expressions, were composed and approved in 1835 by the French king, Louis-Philippe, who could claim his throne thanks to a revolution.)

"When people, in the name of popular supremacy, have turned the state upside down, the removal of all pseudo-freedoms can prove to be very suited to controlling a turbulent sovereign. I know that an iron sceptre becomes the wish and the necessity of a harassed nation."7

But since it does not include the rejection of the revolutionary theories of unbelief, the reaction is nothing more than a revised application of the same theory. They only differ in the end result. "Just as the party of the movement focuses first on freedom before order, so the friends of the reaction focus on order before freedom. They forget that order by revolutionaries can only be gained by giving up freedom. To prevent the repeat of unrest and clashes, people let the minimal remainders of freedom disappear."

"Just as in the past there was fruitless resistance against despotism, rooted in the popular supremacy, so now people are forced to bend before an autocracy that puts the sovereign people in chains (to protect the harassed nation against the recurrence of licentiousness). Some may argue that I borrowed the broad strokes of this image from the oppression of Napoleon. I do not deny that. One recognizes in this oppression not an incidental appearance but the revolutionary line in bent form. Too much popular freedom breeds tyranny."[8]

Groen described this in greater detail when he discussed the habit of the French emperor to appeal to the popular sovereignty. "People have belittled this claim to popular authority as being haughty and a mockery. Not so! The appeal was genuine. It contained the origin of his power. This claim was correct and justified. The people were sovereign, and the emperor was delegated to be the first representative of the people. The supremacy of the people had been carried over by popular will from the bosom of the nation. He possessed it now with equal rights as the complete string of revolutionary governments; with more justification because out of the confusion and misery, the single-person rule appeared now indispensable."[9]

However, reactionary conservatism cannot endure permanently. It is in turn subjected to the law of revolutionary development. "The reaction, even when it has become unavoidable and violent because of the revolution, has a destructive tendency. Whatever she bridles, she torments. She increases the spirit in that which she controls. The reaction is a change for worse, unless in embracing the unchangeable truths of public justice it turns toward anti-revolutionary politics."[10]

Between these two streams of revolution and reaction, develops a third party in the application of the changeover theory. They believe in the theory like the other parties but want to stop the development at their perceived balance point between freedom and order. They desire *le juste milieu*, between *mouvement*—forward movement—and *resistance*—restraint. Groen has put together a description of their goals and the results which show the revolutionary colours in their unity and variety.

Three streams can be identified "wherever the liberal theory is put into action. Three! No more, no less! Take as example the French Revolution in 1789 or 1830 or 1848; research what took place as soon as a new or changed order was established. Check the events in Germany or the Netherlands or anywhere else where revolution theory was put into practice. Study the whole revolution era. Notice the factions that clashed together in each crisis. Throughout the variations in events, one can identify the similarity among political groups.

"It boils down to three groups each time. One party that fears advancement, one party that desires it, and one party that alternatively supports and hinders the movement. To use their familiar names: *la resistance, le movement, le juste milieu*. The first one desires freedom but meets anarchy; the second one searches for order and gets despotism; the third one wants the middle road, which eventually becomes unbearable and impossible."[11] All three belong in the same revolutionary camp.

Toward each other they all hold some measure of justification. "But they all err and deceive because they all persist in the same theory. It is false in its origin and therefore is harmful in its consequences and results. They mill around in an endless circle unless one steps out of the false wisdom into the simple and unchangeable truth of public justice. Without the sovereignty granted by the grace of God, no other authority is conceivable: no royalty, no parliamentary government, no well-ordered republic.

"There is only the revolutionary condition with ordering powers that constantly struggle for change. There is an unavoidable antagonism in which government is powerless (caved in under popular power) or oppressive (maintained by excessive force). While the root of the error is sustained, restoration is unthinkable. It will take a radical change coming from a different root.

"With the best intentions, there will be a change of dictators, who will maintain the oppression. It will still be the despotism of the revolutionary state: the same idolatry of the law, the same denial of the highest Lawgiver and King, the same submission of the church to the state, the same centralization acting as sword and shield of the government and the same arbitrariness applied also to the obtained rights and peculiar independence."[12]

> When we consider Groen's political action in the sphere of state against the background of revolution theory and its application, we can begin to understand its character and intention. It had a two-pronged meaning as expressed in the two names with which he preferred to point out his own direction: *anti-revolutionary*, or directed against the theories of the revolution, and *Christian-historical*, or fighting for its own theory. The content and the application of this theory will be discussed by Groen in the next three chapters.

But first let us consider which form and what influence the revolution theory has had within our Netherlandic borders. We will mostly consider the brushstroke lines without going into exact detail. Just as in all of Europe, so in the Netherlands during the nineteenth century have the revolutionary theories been brought into practice. In 1813, after Napoleon's defeat, they meant indeed a national Netherlandic restoration, and initially the intention was partially realized. "However—pity!—this homeland jurisdiction soon became overwhelmed by a different element. The upper class and all those on whose views the ordering of our interest depended were already influenced by the general European spirit.

"What is the reason, people asked, that after applying enlightened philosophy a series of misfortunes followed? Exaggerating the revolutionary theories allows abuse followed by a strong reaction, which made them powerless. Those principles need to be openly examined with care and precision. A permanent balance can be established everywhere by proper division of state powers, as was done in England. It seemed that the whole of Western Europe turned into a constitution factory. By various combinations, many charters were brought forward that included much of the national forms but submitted to the new revolutionary public justice and thus became lifeless. In that way, theories that had caused twenty-five years of anxiety with almost unchallenged authority gained the upper hand; the condition of unity, the guarantee of permanent happiness, was sought in the perfect application of mild and liberal ideas, and reasoning destroyed sound thought and homeland feelings."[13]

This brought the Netherlands under the influence of liberal thinking, which was no more than "a heartless copy of Jacobinism [a radical branch of revolutionaries that promoted the Reign of Terror and other extreme measures, active chiefly from 1789 to 1794; named from the Dominican convent in Paris, where they originally met. HB] ideas with conformity in principles and meaning." The way was paved for the rule of liberalism, which was nothing more than "radicalism, stopped in its development."[14]

King Willem I, regardless of his good qualities, switched continually with the majority of his administration between liberal and conservative implementations. It looked exactly like enlightened despotism, which is revolutionary in nature. Consequently, "no monarchy was established tempered by independent institutions and real freedoms, [but rather] "a revolutionary superpower resulted, concentrated in the personal will of one single person. The excellence of a governing monarch [when Groen wrote this in 1840, King Willem I had not yet stepped down, HS] nor the love for a ruling House (of Orange) may blind us to the nature of this authority. It is all inclusive and essentially autocratic; it comes down to being self-government, solo ruler in the most literal sense of the word. It is a revolutionary autocracy. The style restrains all essential popular developments because its authority encroaches upon every sphere of society: provinces, church, education and any other administered entity; it governs and regulates large and small business and ultimately controls interests, freedoms and rights—may I say so, arbitrarily."[15]

When the liberals formed the government after 1848, the revolutionary ideas were moved forward into practice. Their leader, Thorbecke, was a strong ruler, just as King Willem I was a powerful regent. Thorbecke may be identified as the inheritor of the king's policies. Thorbecke "was and remained the representative of the revolutionary theory of 1789; *state supremacy* even in *Church and State*." He was both a friend and an enemy of popular sovereignty; a friend because in the anarchy of the popular supremacy lies the focal point of arbitrary reaction and concentrated state supremacy; an enemy because no state power is able to control unbridled advancement of erroneous theory."[16]

In essence, the so-called conservatives were homogenous in theory to Thorbecke and the liberals, regardless of acting as strong opponents. They did not want to go as far and therefore agreed more often with the anti-revolutionaries than with the liberals. When pressed, they were founded on the same revolutionary theories. The liberal-conservatives and the liberal-liberals were, as Groen characterized them so aptly, "constantly squabbling twins in the liberal camp." Their mutual relationship did not determine their demarcation in politics. "The latter with many changes practices the revolution theories; the former continually challenges all forms and 'corrections.'"

In the Netherlands, too, they have appeared unavoidably out of the general development of theories and the nature of the world crisis of our age, even where people are ignorant of actual politics. "Essentially there are only two political streams with a unique theory and an independent presence. These are the *Christian-historical* and the *liberal* (liberal-conservative or conservative-liberal or radical or modern) streams. The one practically applies the Revolution theory, the other opposes all it forms and changes."[17]

What have the liberal theories led to? Just watch church and school. To justify state involvement, the revolutionary theories were applied here too.

"Government was the concentrated People. It was called to take care of all the interests of those it represented. Duties of care gave it the right to control. Complete control was not possible in streamlining the forces of the nation into channels and culverts or by laws and regulations. This function also had to be applied to the most intimate interests of religion and education."[18]

The fruit of this change for the church was a loss of freedom and consequently her powerlessness against encroaching errors. "It is known that in 1816 on the church a type of church order was imposed that was directly in conflict with its confession. Because of this two-faced set up and against the sternest warnings, a liberty in teaching was started that has led to much injustice and confusion."

How was this system established in 1816? "The church had to be renewed according to the state. Even in this sphere, the recommended unity had to be applied that disturbed its natural and free development. It rather concentrated everything in a centre, and except for a few unimportant forms of representation and elections, suppressed it by an artificial system and a dominating leadership.

"Centralization and concentration were the call of the day. The Gereformeerde Kerk was administered as part of the state mechanism and became a department for control. A Ministry for Worship was established, completely in the spirit of the system of administration that was inherited from the French Revolution with its liberal-despotic development. It led to the notion of the state-church in which the teachers as officials and the members as subordinates of the state were considered."[19]

After the new regulations in 1852, this "caesar-like papist yoke" continued. Later the liberals seemed to support more favourably freedom and independence of the church. They took the position that the state had nothing to do with the church. She just would allow it to exist without supporting its influence on the nation.

But "if one does not accept the right of religious denominations to regulate public worship, one embraces the revolutionary system of the *absolute* state with its own religious system or allows idolatry with freedoms that do not interfere with those of the state. It is a state that *tolerates* religious persuasions at its cost and allows the people religious concepts that the government considers sufficient and harmless. This type of religion may be changed at any time with the approval of the government. In essence, it becomes a civil or cultural or political religion of the state, impeding everything that the religious denominations in a nation appreciate."[20]

In terms of *school*, they thought outside of the revolutionary system, namely that the state "has the right and the duty to direct the nation's nurturing based on its own views and insights. It was important to maintain unity of the state and therefore unity of the national educational system. This unity was not possible without uniting the children of all religions in one school system, in spite of objections of the church and conscientious objections of parents." Practically this means "the formation of the nation and civilizing of the next generation according to the mindset and expectations of the government. No one can be allowed to divert from the state-prescribed regulations."[21]

In this context, Groen's struggle for freedom of education was a struggle against the application of revolutionary theory. (This point is here briefly and not further explained.) Correctness of his views was proven in real life. The liberals also supported freedom of education. Therefore, this freedom was guaranteed with the support of Thorbecke in the constitution of 1848.

However, it is clear what happened to this freedom under liberal rule. Because of Thorbecke's "strong influence, this freedom of education succumbed to the fate of all freedoms that make liberalism an illusion and unnoticeable in practice. This happened regardless of elevating this right as one of the most important popular rights guaranteed in the constitution."[22]

Groen did not oppose the state school system as such, neither the universal Christian nor the one neutral in religious character. His attack was directed against the state imposing submission of one's conscience to the revolutionary theories.

CHAPTER 5

The Solid Foundation

"In our present social context, marked by a dramatic struggle between the culture of life and the culture of death, there is need to develop a deep critical sense capable of discerning true values and authentic needs...The culture of life means respect for nature and protection of God's work of creation" (Pope John Paul II).*

Groen had the gift of summarizing complex thought patterns in a synoptic, simple statement. Various of his statements became popular slogans. They were like flashing signs lighting up his speeches. They suddenly showed the heart of a complicated issue clearly. Think, for example, of expressions such as "In our isolation lies our strength" or "It is written, it has been fulfilled" and others like it. The same is true for the slogan, "Instead of the revolution the gospel." It has proven to be the only effective means of opposing the theory of unbelief.

In the Holy Scriptures, Groen found the foundation that provides anchorage in all circumstances. "The Bible is the book among books, especially in the anti-revolutionary bookcase. Modern views, even those that don't openly reject revelation, opine that divine guidelines for public justice are not fitting. In contrast, we defend that Holy Scripture directs us to the foundations of justice and

---

* Pope John Paul II, *Encyclical Evangelium Vitae*, April 1995. Quoted in Vincent Barry, *Bioethics in a Cultural Context.* Cengage Learning, 2011, p. 192

morality, authority and freedom, even for nations and governments. The Bible is the truthful canon. (It is not searchable like an encyclopedia, as some would want us to believe.) Unconditional submission to God's Word has always been the guarantee for disciplined obedience and resistance.

"Beside the truths of Revelation, theories of proud self-fulfillment and gross licentiousness cannot hold. It is written! Notice this axe that cuts every root of revolutionary weeds. The promise of the future does not lie in changing, adjusting or regulating corrupted principles, nor in the lack of effort and deadly acceptance of them. It rests in the declaration of the highest truth, the acceptance of which is the *conditio sine qua non*. Only by cutting out error and supporting the good, passed on by our ancestors, do we find the narrow way that leads to the happiness of nations."[1]

Steadfast belief in the Word of God offers the option of clearly focused resistance to the principles of unbelief, including those for the sphere of the state. It offers the only source for a solution to the constantly recurring problem of the balance between authority and freedom.

The gospel teaches "that every sovereign authority, directly and immediately in origin and guideline, finds its guarantee and limitation in the will of God." (This counts in general for all authority that in its particular sphere is not accountable or submissive to higher human authority.) Therefore, it expects the "unconditional submission of government and people to Him under whose temporary gifts of grace the authority of government and the freedom of nations have been provided."[2]

To make himself clearer, he did not hesitate to use the term *theocracy*, if understood in the meaning he gave it. "We don't desire a theocracy that expects the state to submit to a priesthood or the church. We do not offer a utopia of a cultural society made up of only righteous Christians in which the state would likely dissolve into the church. (Since we recently have suffered under revolution a sad experience of the affiliation of unbelief with lack of government and slavery.) We are reassured of the connection between service of God, which recognizes authority and freedom, and God's supremacy as the foundation of a system of state and law. In that sense, we believe in the possibility, the realization and the necessity of a theocracy."[3]

Usually Groen described his view as the theory of the *droit divin*, the divine right of government. In his lectures in *Unbelief and Revolution*, he has noted his meaning of that term. The characteristic passages in this work have been copied here.

To the question about the meaning of *droit divin,* one finds "the simple and clear answer in the Holy Scriptures...All persons are submitted to the powers instituted over them because there is no power but the power from God (Exodus 9:16; Psalm 62:11; Isaiah 40:26; Luke 5:24; Romans 9:17; 1 Corinthians 2:5, 15:24-28). Powers that exist have been instituted by God." *All power has been instituted by God.*

"We should not weaken that which seems too powerful to us with an insipid explanation that suits us. We may not avoid the intention of these words by referring to the care of Providence, who draws the good out of the evil it tolerates. The powers are not just allowed, they are *of* God: willed, instituted, made holy! That is the only and real meaning of *instituted* (Romans 13:1).

"We ought to be watchful for a wishful explanation of Scripture instigated by misunderstanding or base intentions. *All power* should be understood in its common sense, which in this context also means God's justice and holiness and can be applied to any *lawful* power...*any kind* of lawful power.

"The *droit divin* is not characteristic of a simple form of dominion, it is granted to all forms of government...All power is from God, it is God's *vice-regent,* God's *servant.* This mutual relationship, these opposite, up and down positions, completely fit this theory. We need to obey this instituted power for God's sake, and this power obeys God. 'She is God's servant for your good,' writes the apostle Paul. (Romans 13:1-7). This divine power is a gift of God, which needs to be exercised in His service, to His honour and to benefit others.

"This meaning of authority is the guardian against all other false criteria that people tend to put in first place. Accountable to no one else but God, the sovereign (human ruler) knows that he/she is accountable to God first and foremost. Being master in the sphere of his/her own rights, he/she understands that honouring the rights of others is ordained.

"Ignoring the rights and freedoms of the population causes wavering of the rights of the sovereign. The servant obeys, not out of fear or to please others, but to conform to God's will. He/she is the servant of the eternal King who rules the kings of the earth. That which seems to subdue rather elevates! The obedience, rooted in the submission to God, is now being regulated and limited by the laws of God.

"This obedience is not endowed with its own rights and freedoms. It is founded upon 'Give the Emperor that which belongs to the Emperor' (Matthew 22:15-22). That does not automatically lead to 'Give the Emperor also what does not belong to the Emperor.' It is rather founded upon 'Give God what belongs to God.'

"What else can be said about this foundation of political wisdom? Authority has been established, all arbitrariness has been bridled, obedience ennobled, freedom protected. The declared truth in its manifold applications is the cement of the state structure."[4]

Groen preferred to appeal to the fact that these principles were taught and applied by the Reformation. Others objected by suggesting that they grew out of a completely different principle that caused them to pave the way for the Revolution—namely the principle of freedom. Groen supported the latter but denied the contrast with his theory and its connection with the Revolution theory.

The reformers certainly preached freedom, "but freedom based on *submission* to God's Word and law; submission to every truth gleaned from God's Word; submission to all authority derived from God's authority. He saw this freedom as a fulfilling of duty, a freedom from people's arbitrariness, a way to be obedient to God's will.

"The reformers strived to be free from human traditions, those that contradict the Bible, free of human ordinances that contradict the ordinances of God. They wanted to search God's Word prayerfully, not for the revelation of reason, but to persuade the temerity of the human mind for the higher light of revelation.

"Confessing that all Scripture is God inspired, reformers encouraged the distribution of the Bible in the vernacular for all people. Human wisdom was not the reformers' motivation; rather they trusted the promise of the Holy Spirit. The natural human cannot grasp the gifts of the Spirit of God.

"The Reformation sought freedom; not to bind rulers and governments by law; not to provide political privileges; not to use freedom as a method to block evil; but as servants of God. Freedom to serve God and to confess the Lord. Not a freedom to express and recommend every state of feeling, but a freedom, if government refers to itself as Christian, to observe the teaching of Christ. If this duty is being prohibited, freedom finds other ways to follow one's conscience.

"A Christian knows that only when the Son of God has made one free, is one truly free (John 8:36). Free of the curse of the law, free from the dominion of sin, free of perdition. When referring to earthly powers, he understands the freedom to serve. He knows the freedom to serve God in every relationship. He strives in service to God to be servant and subject to his neighbour too."

Consistent practice followed the teaching. History has demonstrated where the Reformation led. "Among unbelief and rebellion, the Reformation has posed the principle of faith and obedience that brought salvation and order by unifying freedom and submission. This submission to God held up the crumbling authority of government. This submission to God guarded the freedom of the subjects with the shield of holiness blazed by obtained rights. Submission to God stopped the yeast-like effect of Revolutionaries.

"The God-ordained powers proved inviolable as expressed in the proper relation of church to state and in the whole Christian system of public justice."[5] These same principles were the basis for the practice of our forefathers. Groen saw them reflected in the national anthem. Prince Willem van Oranje testified: "Before God I confess and by His mighty power, did I at no time despise the king [of Spain. HB]."

But why, if he did not despise the king, did he take up arms? "As a devout Christian man praised for God's Word, Have I freely, unyielding as a hero, without fearing, exposed my noble blood."

Submitted by his conscience until his conscience was bound. Submitted to the government as servant of God until her orders contradicted God's ordinances: "Then could I obey God the Lord, the highest Majesty, in all righteousness."[6]

Indeed, "in training under the gospel, people learn to be cautious about everything that points to rebellion or cursing the king even in secret. It teaches one to honour the king, because one fears God. When rebellion derails, one learns to continue to submit to the good and humble ruler. When arbitrariness denies freedoms and rights, when flattering praises rebellion, when cowardice prevents disapproval, when despondency bears in suffering, the gospel teaches self-denial, uniting with lawful resistance in word and deed as it is being prescribed in the interest of church and country."[7]

These evangelical principles are completely opposed to the Revolutionary theory—precisely because practicing the gospel delivers while the Revolutionary theory makes vain promises.

"The ideas on which the attraction of philosophy was based originated from Christian roots. They were beneficial when they were connected to the gospel but turned destructive after they had been separated. Christian love generates true *humanity* and recognizes *human rights,* including those of the least, without discrimination of race, colour, ancestry or class." Reality has proven "that only the gospel holds the true principles of freedom, equality, brotherhood, philanthropy and beneficial humanitarianism."[8]

Revolution is anti-historical: the gospel respects the historical development because it takes into account God's rule and laws. It is wise to be careful with

Rejoice! Sing Praise to Your Creator*

1
Rejoice! Sing praise to your Creator,
For it is good to praise the Lord.
Make music with guitar and trumpet;
Blend skillfully each note and word.
All God's words are truthful.
All his works are faithful.
He loves righteousness.
To the earth and heavens
Constant care is given
With unfailing love.

2
God spoke his word to make the heavens:
His spirit gave the stars their birth.
He gathers all the ocean's waters
In storehouses around the earth.
Who should not adore him,
Stand in awe before him?
What he spoke was done:
Place and life were given
To seas, earth and heaven.
Let all fear the Lord!

3
The Lord upsets the plan of nations;
He frustrates all that they devise.
But God's own plan stands firm forever,
And all his purposes are wise.
Blessed is that nation,
Every generation
For whom God is Lord.
Bound to him forever,
Nothing now can sever
God from those he chose.

4
The Lord on high looks down from heaven;
He sees all people he has made.
No king is saved by might or army;
A warrior's horse will not give aid.
Our Lord sees with favour
Those who love their Saviour—
Keeps his eye on them.
Death's bonds he will sever,
Save their lives forever—
God will save from death.

5
Our souls wait for the Lord, our keeper;
He is our help, he is our shield.
Shout loudly, praise the Lord, and trust him
Who has our life and future sealed.
God, our loving Saviour,
Keeps us safe forever.
Holy is his name!
God the Lord is loving,
Always, always proving
God will save from death

* Words: Psalm 33: The Sovereignty of God in Creation and History (NKJV); vers. Marie J. Post (1919-1990), 1980, © 1987, Faith Alive Christian Resources. Music: Genevan Psalter, 1551; harm. Claude Goudimel, 1564, alt., P.D. Used with permission.

conclusions, yet to the Christian, when considered in the light of God's Word, history can be a fulcrum.

The unity of Scripture and history and their combined protest against the Revolution theory were touched on by Groen in his foreword to *Unbelief and Revolution*: "I finish with the declaration, against all human wisdom and with a feeling of my own inability, that there is a guarantee of victory in the slogan *It is written* and *It has happened!*

"It is a guarantee against any attack, a root against any turmoil of philosophical unbelief. History is also the glowing record of the Holy God. Holy Scripture itself is a historical record in which events and instructions are inseparable. History is a continuing testimony not only in its listing of factual deeds but especially in the formation and development of ideas. History confirms its origin, meaning, direction and unity in the facts of revelation.

"The Holy Scriptures reveal the law through Bible study; it shames, in the foolishness of the cross, the finely crafted wisdom of philosophers and sages with a devout, childlike faith; it testifies of the Lamb that has been slain; it shares the prophecy of the shoot from Jesse's stump and the victorious Lion from the tribe of Judah. It tells about the Son of David and David's Lord, divine and human, Mediator and Judge, who after offering the staff of grace without getting a response, holds the iron sceptre for destruction of His stiff-necked opponents. History and Holy Scripture point the penitent sinner, under a forfeited blessing of perseverance beyond human calculation, the way to Him who with the glow of His perfections has revealed Himself among the Netherlandic population too."[9]

CHAPTER 6

The Christian's Calling

O nly in the gospel lies the solid foundation against the theories of unbelief. Note well: in the *living* gospel. Dead orthodoxy has never been a resistance against the influence of this error. To the contrary, it tends to foster the error. It showed in the Netherlandic history of the eighteenth century. "A cold orthodoxy, after loss of its lively testimony, looked for support in every type and detail of outward system. It was powerless against immorality and doubt. It now prepared the way for the theories that caused submission of religion to reason. Its authority was designed on the arbitrary choices of humans."[1]

The confession of the gospel truth, if it is to be powerful, needs to flow from the heart as the fruit of a devout and childlike faith. That expectation is for every Christian regardless of their position or degree. "One thing I know and confess. One thing is needed for everyone. Not as officials or professors, but as sinners do we receive salvation. There is one way, one truth. I find rest and peace for my soul in the joyful message that gracious forgiveness through the sufficient sacrifice of the Saviour is offered to everyone who believes."

These "evangelical truths, whose necessities were never better understood than in times of lack, are no mysteries that will be introduced by a deep or flighty human philosophy but revealed by God to the lowly and meek. These truths are clearly as well as simply expressed in the Scriptural narrative."[2] Participation in these truths is not only a privilege but also a responsibility. There are upright gospel confessors who believe that Christ will maintain His

71

church and then conclude that He does not need weak sinners to see His truth become victorious.

However, Groen suggests "that they forget that the Lord does not need our participation to be victorious but desires it. His excellent power has been hidden in earthly vessels." (2 Corinthians 4:7.)

"Christ's Almighty power and the certainty of His victory is being declared as a reason to be steadfast, unmovable, always abundantly involved in the work of the Lord. Our work in the Lord is never useless. The question is not if the Lord will be victorious but rather if those who saw the Kingdom under attack will be victorious with Him. Or will they neglect to battle and join peacefully with His enemies?"3

Certainly, one thing is necessary. "When we possess that one thing, its fruits can be evident in everything. As far as salvation of souls is concerned, we want to know nothing but Christ crucified. When we know Him, the awareness of His love may revive and stir us everywhere He can be honoured. The proclamation of the gospel is everyone's responsibility to whom it has been made known. This declaration to all creatures can take place in various ways. No means may be left idle that can penetrate the human mind or mood."4

For the fulfillment of this calling, it is primarily necessary to deepen our own conviction by continual study of the principles. "The Christian incorrectly may assume that besides the guidelines of Scripture he does not need scholarship. To work diligently and accurately in every opportune connection, he needs to understand clearly the nature and the demands of his own task. 'The fear of the Lord is the beginning of knowledge' (Psalm 111:10; Proverbs 1:7). But the beginning is not the complete scholarship. It is being formed from all other parts which embody the principle."

"The evangelical truth is the yeast. When baking nutritious and tasty bread, the yeast requires dough to make a loaf. The dough of scholarship is needed in order to present sound reasoning. May our idleness not be a deceptive excuse for the all-sufficiency of God's Word. This leads to a form of tempting God. Can one expect to be saved by a Christian instinct, with practical issues of public justice, when evil is called good and good evil?" Is it wise to dig into all interpretations of issues or "become involved in practical battles to prevent the implementation of opinions that we perceive as damaging?" Groen advises: "Certainly, it is beneficial and responsible to know now as well as later not only the scope of issues but especially the roots and the *branching out* of evil. To understand the error, the cure may be found more readily.

"With an infallible Christian scholarship, we may be steadfast and remain unmoved against the wind of many theories. Consequently, when we defend the truth we do not become guilty of listening to doubtful opinions, which make the true testimony of a witness often powerless."[5]

Only this foundational understanding leads to strength of conviction. Partial knowledge leads to compromises and doubt, which causes agreement with the error that is hidden in the phantom of truth. When Groen analyzes the causes of the retreat of Christian thought and action in the Netherlands after 1813, he declares, "It is because the gospel truth has been banned from state and church, school and home. More correctly it is being faked. People accepted relative gospel truths, which were being conformed to the demand of the circumstances and state formations.

"Soon fallacies in religion and politics were stretched, shaped and softened. The Christian went along with that which he should have resisted. They respected a forced peace with everyone and everything. They had forgotten that when the gospel has been doused of life in the believer's heart, it can live in peace with error. No form of devotion, no half gospel, no gospel comfortable to all, no gospel declaration that everyone brags about, no gospel that gives one peace with everybody, no gospel that denies and makes a caricature of the teaching of salvation can offer that which people need for essential and enduring salvation of the nations. No wavering confessing instituted the church in our countries. No insecure confessing established her and the Netherlandic state and protected her through immense dangers and used her for immeasurable blessing."[6]

Knowledge alone is not sufficient. It needs to be accompanied by action that purposes to implement confessed truths. Self-examination is fitting for the Christian. Circumstances may be of such a nature that the application of his principles in practice is being made impossible. Not always are the circumstances the cause for this. The fault could lie with the confessors of the principles, for example, when "the will is lacking to put them into practice. Is the latter the cause among us?

"Christians have been accused, rightly or wrongly, of self-aggrandizing. It is certain that when the heart becomes proud, the truth leads to humiliation. As we become more knowledgeable, the contrast between knowing and doing shows more sharply. The more strength is displayed in the confession, so its failure will likely point more to the confessor."[7]

Groen understood history well enough to know that circumstances can indeed prevent the practical application of principles. That is "if we understand under practical a speedy and advantageous victory for ourselves. However, under unfavourable circumstances, truthful witnessing can continue. This ongoing witness is a powerful practice in itself. The preaching of the truth is not redundant during times of unrighteousness."[8]

By defending their principles, Christian citizens are not only faithful to their calling but serve their country too. "It is always important for a state to have citizens that sacrifice because of their principles. I mean this in general; when a principle is erroneous, correction and, if necessary, restraint may be demanded. A country may call itself blessed when there are those who have a higher purpose than self-interest and are willing to sacrifice or be persecuted for it. It is good when truthful citizens all have been driven away; rest may likely follow. However, it would be a rest that would usurp the homeland as a rust."[9]

The type of resistance needs to be *principled*. It is not focused on people, but on ideas. Our judgment concerning opponents needs to be fair. "Considering our own weakness, we do well to be cautious in our judgment of other *persons*. They are easily pulled along by ideas, of which they underestimate their harmful nature. It is not easy to distance oneself from bad influences when the error is widely accepted. An irresistible flow of events does not remove personal responsibility. Nobody has to bend the knee for the idol of the age. One will not be judged for the impossibility of resistance but rather for the willingness to cooperate."

However, "there exists an atmospheric intoxication in responsibility comparable to involuntary drunkenness. A cool attitude among a general excitement is unusual."

"People are ready to blame writers and leaders of the revolution, like Montesquieu, Voltaire and Rousseau, for idolatry and rebellion, and Robespierre and Napoleon for anarchy and despotism. Indeed, in as much as word and deed count, a great deal of the responsibility rests with them; however, they also were agents of the spirit of the times. Writers expressed in words that which people in general already had accepted; interpreters rather than teachers of public opinion; teachers only in that they advanced one more step, outside of which no stopping was possible.

"The same counts for the powerful of the revolution. They are carried on the wings of the spirit of the times, wrapped in its direction, first forerunners then leaders following a track voluntarily followed by everyone else. They are leaders being led, driven on and pushed forward. It is important to keep this in mind in order not to overly blame their character or praise their talents excessively. It helps to understand their nature, their context and their strength of the error. Evaluating them requires considering their contemporaries, who may be fearful of extremes, yet adhering to the theory. They are not only responsible for the error and its practice but also for the string of errors and practices that followed from the theory."[10]

Since the battle is not focused on people but on principles, it is important that the Christian seeks cooperation with everyone who accepts the truth of the gospel. Disunity among Christians weakens the resistance. "Against unbelief all of Christendom stands, united by faith in the one sacrifice, fulfilled once on the cross." That unity needs to be sought and encouraged, strengthened and consciously planned. "The revolutionary theory affects all of Christendom. Reformers, Lutherans and adherents of the Church of Rome are all equally under threat. The defense needs to be communal."

"Not by a forced unity or approach, as often has been seen in revolutionary times, which in fact is a concession of indifference and unbelief, but by conviction of the Christian faith; by a rightly driven rejection of a theory. It would have a negative outcome if this unity were used against other Christians for serving oneself. It should be a vivid awareness that the difference among denominations in which Christ is worshipped as Lord and Saviour is much less than that between Christendom and a theory in which atheism is enveloped."[11]

Considering this argument, as an example, Groen sought cooperation with Roman Catholics, although he did not spare them his criticism. Long before it was practiced in actual situations, he already proposed that "in the Netherlands, believing Protestants and Roman Catholics could work together." He recommended "strict observance of denominational principles but a common front in the political and constitutional sphere against unbelief, radicalism and the revolutionary supremacy of the state. It essentially threatens the rights and faith of all denominations."[12]

In this way, the fulfillment of the calling of the Christian citizens reaches into the area of politics. Can they remain idle when the state changes their expression of faith in church and school? It is understood that "the Christian submits himself to the monarchy, the democratic, republican as well as aristocratic form of government. However, he is obligated to witness against a theory which in its nature and conclusion goes against the ordinances and supremacy of the living God. He can live under any form of government. But he should make use of the rights available to him in that form of government—be it understood that their use would not be conditional nor conflict with the faithfulness to his own principles."

"If, as in 1795 and later, a political confession for citizenship had to be signed, it would be objectionable. However, when revolutionaries have no objection for others to participate, there would be no excuse to remain idle when one can participate without signing onto the revolutionary principles. One should make use of the existing and lawful forms. When the Apostle Paul claimed the rights of Roman citizenship in Philippi (Acts 16:37-40), he did not approve the form of government, even less so the adopted principle of arbitrary choices and oppression. Long suffering suits the Christian; however, when the opportunity for cooperation exists, suffering is not appropriate."[13]

Continually, Groen held this idea up to his compatriots who posed that religion and politics should remain separate. He summarized their and other views like this: "Religion, as people readily admit, is good, excellent, and indispensable in life and death. It is the foundation of morality and much more. However, one needs to recognize religion in its proper place just like everything else and in that context reference it. Religion suits the communal gathering for worship and family customs. Keep it in church and home."

"It is mistaken and essentially a disservice to the issue one hopes to advance when one continually uses the recommendation of religious principles as arguments in politics. Just because of the necessity of *pia vota* in the usual sense of unfulfillable desires, heaven is brought into a special and forced relationship with the earth."[14]

Groen called this attitude "politicophobia," that is, the disposition "that shudders to think of the evangelical witness in politics." This outcry denies the calling of the Christian. "Certainly, it is an atrocity to make religion submissive to politics. It is equally irresponsible to withdraw oneself from the maintenance of rights, which are indispensable in the fulfilment of Christian duties, with the excuse that one has no heart for *politics,* out of laziness or wretched twisting."[15]

Against this attitude, which was quite prevalent among his colleagues of the upper class who made his struggle so difficult, Groen posed the proper insight to his followers among the common folk [kleine luyden, HB]. "The instinct for Christian unity reveals itself to the worker as well as the statesman. The *religious* issues, the conscience questions, relevant under the *political* umbrella, are often better perceived among the lowest class in society, because they look for wisdom in the Holy Scriptures."

They understand that it is one and the same battle that is being fought in every area of life, namely the battle against unbelief. Because "this is unbelief by which the human will and wisdom elevate themselves above God's laws and revelation. It has in practical ways penetrated every sphere and branch of society. Therefore, resistance in every social sphere and multiplicity of structures to the same enemy is a duty."

"In the global frame that we experience and, according to prophecy, expect, it is more important than ever to be united in our view of the contrast between belief and unbelief, religion and idolatry. We need to see all great or small human endeavours tied to one obligation and one God-honouring struggle."[16]

Religion and politics cannot be separated. Those who try to do it forget that "Christians are not called to a narrow-hearted, follow-the-rules religion, ignoring the important cultural issues that cannot be resolved without their powerful participation." Is one only focused on keeping the church confessions? Experience shows "that every religious party whose faith is being disrupted in the church or oppressed by the state, as result of diligent defense of truth and righteousness, does not *bastardize* into but *reveals* itself as an ecclesiastical body and as a political party. Self-interest, ambition and injustice may be mixed in with the activities of this party but they appear in all human activities.

"A religious conviction loses its power when it does not, in support of that which it confesses as truth, use the means available in the interest of church and state. History shows that the accomplishments of ecclesiastical-political parties often show the power of human virtue and godly blessings. An ecclesiastical party instituted the jurisdiction of the United Netherlands...Here and elsewhere an ecclesiastical party significantly elevates the true civil and political freedom by a simple devout faith that by other ways and means obstinately and fruitlessly is being sought."[17]

Those who have come to understand this connection want to testify principally in politics, even though a quick solution may be excluded and objections may be their results. In the postscript to his friends who followed his reading of *Unbelief and Revolution,* Groen remarked: "Even in unfavourable circumstances, witness can be done; this constant witness is a powerful practice...I may not avoid the answer to the question what I think of the present circumstances: I do not consider them favourable. Vain hope and petty visions don't help. It is unnecessary to repeat that we live in a period of decline—a crisis. Healing of this cancerous sphere may not be expected in the short term."

"We cannot promise a complete, speedy, easy triumph. Nobody should get involved with anti-revolutionary politics if he desires the wellbeing of the country merely by walking along the way in which a person finds satisfaction for his own desires and interests. If one dislikes such a narrow spiritual view, let it be clear that there is ample opportunity to practice diligence."

"Or is the witness to principles a negligent responsibility? Do you believe that not only in the documents but also in the discussions of the eighteenth century, minimum power was displayed for the revolution? In one's willing testimony of convictions is a power only known by Him who gives the growth."

"Some will suggest that enough has been spoken and written. Now it is time to act! Is speaking and writing not acting? Did the sower in Jesus' parable swing an empty hand? (Matthew 13:3-9, 18-23.) I recognize that the encouragement also has a healthy and important meaning. It directs us not to stay with visions when practice is allowed. Let us be faithful and everyone keep watch.

"Let us be aware that if no great things can be done now, the negligence of the small things could display the greatest unfaithfulness. If preaching can be called *deed,* the deed also *preaches.* Let us focus on duty and self-denial even when the minutest sacrifices are required of us right now. Let us remember that the dominion of truth has been spread by witnesses who had the conviction to testify when necessary unto death. In the practical sense, they became martyrs."[18]

For those who witness with a self-denying perseverance, there waits an inherited reward. "What can be more glorious for a Christian than to experience a bit of 'the zeal for Your house has eaten me up' (Psalm 69:9; John 2:22)? What could be more glorious for the Christian, by obedience in their own life choices, than to experience the simple manifested expression of the Benedicts, the burning candle with the inscription *Terar dum prosim* (let me be consumed if only I may be useful)."[19]

Specific Examples
PART III

CHAPTER 7

Groen's Example:

DEVELOPMENT IN THE NETHERLANDS

A. CONNECTION WITH THE NATION'S PAST

Groen van Prinsterer used "State Renewal in Patriotic Context" as a chapter heading in his publication that contributed to the renewal of the Netherlandic constitution. It was fitting for him to suggest this connection because Groen was a staunchly loyal Netherlander. It was one of the reasons he took on the battle against the revolutionary zeitgeist (spirit of the times). At an early stage, he realized that it was both anti-Christian and un-Netherlandic.

With clear intention, he named his periodical, which introduced his career as an anti-revolutionary writer, *Nederlandsche Gedachten* (*Netherlandic Reflections*). It was established under the pressure of the revolutionary unrest in the south of the Netherlands. This was the early instigation of the Belgian rebellion.

In the principled statement and situational description that introduced the paper, Groen wrote: "Already for some time the south of the kingdom has been mostly dominated by one outspoken, dangerous faction; a milder expression may not be used." This minority, which envisioned the French model, "at the same time endangered the constitutional throne, Protestantism and the unique Netherlandic character. For various reasons and in a matter of a few months, the attackers gained so much power and daring that they clearly endangered freedom and order, Christian tolerance and independent patriotism."

When will the goal of these "opponents of all that is Netherlandic have been accomplished? Likely when kingdom and nation are subjected to France or at least to French influence. Not everyone who has been caught up in this movement harboured these felonious intentions; but the most fanatical ones had this in mind. This is the application of already openly preached principles: sovereignty of the people and unlimited freedom, which is essentially a theory that does not respect the freedom of others. It results in a denial of the Netherlandic principles that are the foundation of the Netherlandic state. Never has a faction willingly rested until it has become completely victorious. Once the theories take hold, people are dragged along against their own will to the extreme consequences."

Groen counters this movement by calling upon an awakening of a *patriotic* spirit. "Which means are effective enough to sidetrack this danger? The revival of a truly Netherlandic spirit. It resists licentiousness and hates oppressive dependence. Informed by pure Christian teaching, one is equipped against unbelief and indifference as well as superstition and fanaticism. In many ways, being attached to the ancestral heritage has clearly identifiable, honourable characteristics that are not easily replaced with the French mode. Only a revival and a continually roused patriotic spirit is a sufficient means for government and people to thwart the enemies of order, true religion and Netherlandic identity."[1]

Throughout his life, Groen has been faithful to this approach. We already observed that he blamed the revolution for always breaking with the past. As promoter of historic thinking, Groen demanded respect for that which had culturally developed already. A political model, which can be applied anywhere and is suitable for every nation, only exists in the whims of the revolutionaries. A nation is more than a "number of souls," more than an incidental gathering of individuals; rather it is the result of historic development that shaped its unique character, distinguishable from all other nations.

The revolutionaries like to play with the words *nation* and *homeland*. "Connecting these words to revolutionary theory, revolutionary interests, revolutionary freedoms and revolutionary citizenship is not helpful. What is a nation, what does homeland mean when one destroys the continuation of the unity of history, religion, traditions, customs, principles from ancestors to descendants?"[2]

The revolution theory denies the origin of the popular power because in essence "it breaks with history even though it borrows from earlier situations that which suits its ideas. It does not feel itself bound in any way with historic development. A nation, in its unity of ancestors to descendants, is not unlike a tree that feeds all branches and every twig in its crown from the roots. Cut the root systematically with an axe, and soon one can make a paling with the dead branches. It is no longer the tree that repeatedly grows leaves, blossoms and fruit that are the living testimony to the power of the roots."[3]

Therefore, in the Netherlands, as in every other country, the only redeeming politics is the one that connects with its patriotic traditions. This is true for those who appreciate a continuing natural national development. "No nation is free unless it is governed according to the principles of its *historic* human existence."

Is it not true "that a free people cannot distance themselves from the natural law of their formation that connects them to their origin and development? They do not have the choice in their own nature and historic character. A nation has not created itself, just as a human being has not formed itself; it is bound to its individual identity. Its nationality expresses the unique identity of a nation."[4]

For this reason, Groen warned in 1829 to break with the Belgians over that which had become a cultural possession in the northern provinces. "Let's say it with confidence while it is still possible—one cannot force a people who feel worthy to adopt regulations foreign to its traditions, foreign to the naturally developed constitution. They cannot tolerate the theft of traditions that are woven in their national identity. These have been received from their ancestors, and they hope to pass them onto their children as an inheritance of real cultural happiness."[5]

It is important that its state structure conforms to the historically developed unique character of the people. "In a way, the structure of the state is for the nation what the body is for the soul. It is the organ by which it operates. It is the figure in which it receives its development and reveals its maturity. Not arbitrarily but naturally and necessarily does it connect with the unique characteristics of the population."

Therefore, Groen maintains, "there is no nation in which its organic life does not show its own unique state regulation and display its historic constitution. With the desire for a written constitution, the task of the lawgivers is not to engineer something to please themselves. Rather they should record the foundational characteristics imprinted in the nature of the people when they construct institutions and obtained rights. Preparing reforms that are necessary or desirable should be done respecting these foundational rights. They should pay attention to possible obstacles that hinder the ongoing development and free movement of the nation."[6]

When these observations are being applied to the Netherlands, it means "that the Netherlandic peculiarity, which is rooted in its popular history and popular faith, is its only sufficient guarantee for national flourishing and strength. There is no other way out than a *return to Christian, historic, Netherlandic principles*. When a political movement does not conform, it is likely anti-national since it removes from the Nation that which is critical in its true formation and strength."[7]

Where does one find these national characteristics and Netherlandic principles? According to Groen, "they are written on the hearts of the unspoiled people of the population. Search for them on every page of its history and one can find them everywhere when the people showed spirit and purpose, displayed a greatness of character and influenced other nations for good and especially when the Netherlandic people passed on their Netherlandic reputation unspoiled to the next generation."[8]

Groen considered the study of the national history so important and kept himself occupied long and intensely with it. Knowledge of the nation's story is not only a source for love of country, but also a condition for the maintenance of true Netherlandic being and the defense against anything that goes against it. "One cannot love country, one cannot be a patriot without knowing its history. When people cannot highly appreciate their nation and the relation with its ancestors is not maintained, priority is given to their own customs, own traditions, own literature and even their own independent existence. They will be attracted to strange and new ideas. Along with this new preferred desire, the love for the honour of the nation dwindles and with it the honourable spirit, which was constantly the cause of something great and good. Its history can give new impulse to this weakening pride. A nation's history, more so than money or property, connects the land and its people. A nation's history makes us feel passionate as we participate in the fate and glory of our beloved homeland and appreciate the attraction for everything national."[9]

B. SUSTAINABLE IMPROVEMENTS, NOT REACTIONS

Did Groen demand the past to recur when he called for national politics that connect with the nation's historic foundations? Did it mean that he desires a return to conditions that have passed? Absolutely not! He was blamed many times for this, but he always testified about his disapproval of reaction. He wanted to be known not as contra-revolutionary but as anti-revolutionary.

He referred to the accusation as a caricature when people blamed him and his followers "that we desire the past, only the past, and nothing but the past. As if we don't pay attention to changing circumstances, nor to obtained rights, nor to the development of the science of politics. They accuse us of only being interested in a restoration sloganeered as "*est quia fuit.*" I constantly have turned myself away from going into that direction. I don't deny the revolution, nor the consequences of the revolution, but I reject the revolutionary theories. I view the total cultural development, including the consequences of the revolution as they have developed unto today.

"In my assessment, state and society, in their current situation and form, need to be subjected to the redeeming and sanctifying influence of the unchanging and highest truth. When I am eyeing restoration, my intention is not to bring back outdated ways. I am not thinking of a sudden turnaround of societal conditions, nor a denial of the popular rights, to please one faction.

"Rather, led by experience and taught by the eternally consistent revelation of the Word, I defend the consistence of truths. Their neglect has led to heresies that continually demonstrate powerlessness and depravity. Current application of Christian jurisprudence, updated with the times because of changing circumstances, is needed more than ever."

This application will account for the effects of the revolution. Groen was convinced "that out of the application of revolutionary foolhardiness, theories and institutions of great value would appear. These institutions should not be turned upside down but purified from the revolutionary theories and brought into agreement with the existing history and rights."[10]

However, such a change had to happen slowly and sustainably. Groen posed "that a change or reformation, to be truly reforming and enduring, should be established. This cannot be done in a hurry and unconditionally, but rather slowly and with respect for what already exists."[11]

Therefore, he warned against speeding ahead. One should be quite assured that the new improves on the old before continuing. "To change for the sake of change without improvement and without guarantee for succeeding when in the action no difficulties can be perceived is not of value."[12]

Groen expected less blessing from forceful action to bring about reformation. "I am against force and the display of force. I decry it as disallowed and superfluous. To reform a state, especially when the population understands its obligations and rights, requires no force but the awakening of a patriotic spirit and the development of true citizenship." Striving to bring about reforms like this, "maintenance and improvements are the choice rather than destruction and reconstruction. The contemporary needs to be built on the developments from the past.[13]

"It is important not to forget that improvements cannot be a patchwork: now here then there, making changes without considering the unity of the whole. A solid, long-term plan should be followed rather than responding to the necessity of the moment. The salvation of the Netherlands cannot be expected from a favourable run of events but from that which transcends them."[14]

C. CHRISTIAN-NATIONAL

Intense study of our history taught Groen what the national heritage of the Netherlands consists of. He summarized it with two characteristics: *its intimacy with Christendom* and *its sense of freedom*. We will follow how Groen described these traditional characteristics in more detail and how he wanted to see them maintained.

First, *intimacy with Christendom*. Historically considered, the Netherlands is a Christian country. Groen defended that as follows: "When considering our history, it is important to notice that the greatness of the united Netherlands was intimately connected to the blossoming of the Reformed Christian Church (Hervomde Christelijke Kerk). Historical truth, which never has been doubted, is that it existed before history became the servant of predominantly unchristian theories.

"The Netherlands rose up out of its defense of the faith. Godliness has been the dominating and shaping feature of the national character, whose uniqueness and excellence connects directly to this important characteristic. The blossoming and the reputation of the republic can be explained by the energy that the believers brought to social life. This includes regulations to settle church differences as well as the wars with Spain and France, both of which were meant to confirm pure Christian Protestantism. Religion was, just as earlier everywhere else, the foundation of the state. Over time it infiltrated all areas of society. Especially under the banner of the Reformed (Gereformeerd) faith—liberality, tolerance, wealth, national power and greatness were richly evident."[15]

This intimacy to pure Christendom, the reliance on God's Word, was the strength from which the ancestors received endurance and energy. "When we desire to appreciate the courage and the endurance of our Calvinistic ancestors, let us recognize the source of their excellence in their undoubting faith. Because they feared God, for His sake they were undaunted in their fear of worldly powers. Let us recognize that their inner strength was fed by food for the soul—by God's Word. It resisted baseness as well as haughtiness. Let us declare that their courage on battlefields and in courts and even on the stake can be explained by them being equipped with the sword of the Spirit, the Bible, with which they applied the commandments of God to other mortals, without holding back in danger or fearing any danger, based on the promise: 'Be faithful unto death and I will give you the crown of life' (Revelation 2:10).[16]

"This Reformed (Gereformeerd) faith, based on the interpretation of the Calvinistic and Puritan theology, has been the support of the church and state in every tense situation. The Reformed (Gereformeerd) section of the population was not powerful because of its numbers (for an extensive period they were a small minority), but they formed the heart of the nation by their undeniable courage and endurance based on an undoubting faith and acceptance of duty and responsibility."[17]

Even though over time that power of faith weakened, yet the connection to Christendom in the Netherlands is national. Every authentic Netherlandic change in jurisprudence, being truly Netherlandic, took this connection into account. Maintaining the gospel, "the most wonderful heritage of the nation, is not concerned about the outer form, nice words and declarations, a name sign of a corporation, rather we are concerned about a state that continues to be holy, just like the holy covenant of the past. We expect more than now and then a few token phrases toward the loving governance of a wise Providence, woven in state ceremonies. No, we desire something more.

"The national faith is the Christian faith, the national school is the Christian school, the national law giving is the Christian law giving. The Netherlands is a *Christian* country in which obedience to the gospel is a right and a duty for state and citizens. Government, whether Christian or not, is bound to this highest law. *A Christian country!*

Everyone who is bothered by the word *state* recognizes sooner rather than later that under every type of state, the government ought to be aware of the rights and needs of a *Christian nation*. We don't desire the submission of the state to the church. Should the separation be understood in such a way that the denominations as sects, in as far as they agree with public interest and public service, should be *tolerated* within the sphere of their unique institution? No! No separation of church and state by which the nation is robbed of its religion in public regulations. Separation of church and state does not mean that in public regulations in which religion is natural and fitting, the theology of different denominations of which the nation is composed cannot be applied. It is important to recognize the faith of the nation."[18]

However, if one takes the position, which Groen felt he had to take himself later in life, that the state essentially has become faithless, he demanded that it really should practice neutrality; not a forced Christendom over denominations, by which the state would damage scriptural Christendom. Because "in the faithless state are Christians, and I request for them the exercise of liberty necessary for living in Christian responsibility. If public institutions have lost the Christian character, it is still necessary to provide complete liberty for the individual's faith development. It will maintain the Christian voice of the nation and recognizes its history, even though it is not homogenous with the un-Christian state. This voice may not be snuffed out by intentional and multi-sided suppression."[19]

D. PRO LIBERTATE

If intimacy to Christendom is the first traditional Netherlandic characteristic, the second one for our people is the *sense of freedom*. The two connect. "Because of a rock-solid faith in the Word of God, the nation established and maintained freedom and independence. The fact that the 'virgin' Netherlands leaned on Holy Scripture is not just a glorified lesson and a focused allegory on an earlier coin ['God's Breath Scattered Them' was the phrase on a memorial coin specially minted to remember the defeat of the Spanish Armada on June 1, 1588, which was on its way to subdue the Netherlands and Britain under Spanish rule. HB], it is a concise summary of the history of our country."[20]

The term *freedom* demands a closer look. Freedom is of course a slogan that every political movement uses on its banner. The Revolution promised it, too. Groen already explained what happened in practice to this revolutionary freedom. It turned out to be equal to anarchy and licentiousness. However, the uniquely Netherlandic patriotic freedom had a different character. How could our country gain the honourable designation *the classic country of freedom?* "When one truthfully looks at history, it cannot be denied that despite whatever means of defense and self-preservation have been employed during the years as Republic, and compared to what happened in other countries with believers, the Netherlands was *an example of tolerance.*"21

This tolerance has been above all the result of a freedom of conscience. From history, regardless of existing maladministration, we learn that "for our people freedom of conscience was always the most important. In the Netherlands, there was yet unknown freedom for all denominations to live quietly and peacefully as neighbours according to their belief. It made the Netherlands known as a classic country of freedom. Freedom of conscience in this country has been defended against foreign powers, which often banded together in their attack: for example, defended against Spain, against Austria, against France and England in unison. Because this battle for freedom of conscience has been defended with courage and endurance in our country, the Netherlands was named the classic country of freedom! From the Netherlands, in order to limit the suppression of conscience, support has been given abroad. From the Netherlands, under the flag of the Netherlands and the House of Orange, strong support has been offered to England in establishing a state regulation, which maintained true political and religious freedom and which survived numerous liberal state regulations. It established the Netherlands as the classic county of freedom in England and other nations of Europe."

How did it continue to develop? "This national Netherlandic politics of righteousness, tolerance, freedom of conscience for all—did we give it up after we were counted among the classic countries of *liberalism*? Liberalism has had a considerable negative influence on our people. It emancipated the Church of Rome, but in a manner in which they and other denominations were put under the dangerous supremacy of the almighty state. Consequently, so much injustice occurred to all denominations and caused damage to the nation that was felt for years. However, in this liberal atmosphere, the notion of right and truth constantly surfaced. The nature of the classic country of freedom has not been denied."22

Maintaining "this most precious popular right, the freedom of conscience to observe evangelical responsibilities" was for Groen the most important task of national state development, including the maintenance of the rights to liberty that closely connect with it. Groen saw "an unbreakable connection between freedom of conscience, freedom of religious practice and freedom of education." These historically obtained popular rights "have been grafted into its popular memory over the centuries. They form the stable Netherlandic constitution, of which every following constitution should be a copy."[23]

The freedom of religious practice, as a recognized Netherlandic principle, was defended by Groen at a time when the current government denied it to the breakaway reformers (Afgescheidenen). "A communal clinging to the saving gospel, for which the blood of its ancestors flowed, was blindly identified as a crime. Communal and prayerful reading of Holy Scriptures, which taught the government and its people in early days that they did not in vain depend upon the Bible, was now listed with the worst vices."

Generally, Groen defended the freedom and independence of the church and the right of denominations to organize and worship in their own unique way. He wrote that "in this country, the existing Christian denominations, including the Jewish community, have not only a constitutional but also a public and historic presence...The churches in their various denominations are independent corporations within the state. This has various important consequences. First, any apparent *jus in sacra* cannot survive. Second, the church as an independent corporation is allowed to conduct its own unique administration and own business, which naturally belong to it; for example, the freedom to offer Christian education and the complete independence of *diaconal services.* Third, these corporations have a right to receive the same *protection* from government that is offered to all persons and corporations. The church receives it, similar to all other corporations, based on its *peculiar* church character."[24]

Groen strongly identified the limits to freedom of education as an unnational action and an effort to limit freedom of conscience. From those limiting this freedom he asked, "Who gives you, in a free Netherlands, the right to force others? The *question* is not, 'When conscience is an issue, who is right from a religious or irreligious point of view?' Rather the *question* is, 'Does one side have to be silent to that which another side claims right?'" Already in 1840, he stated in the Second Chamber: "Parents who by intuition or well-founded argument in their conscience are convinced that the character of education in the existing educational system is unchristian should not be prevented from offering their children an education consistent with their conscience before God. This force, I declare it resolutely, is unacceptable and has to end. It is another example of the revolution theory, which bypasses the rights of parents and treats their children as property of the state. This freedom of education that I have identified and its companion, freedom of conscience, cannot be denied for long."[25]

This freedom, "as a unique fruit of the Netherlandic love for freedom and understanding of faith" is a national right. "It is about a *right*, not a favour. The nation has the right, based on the guarantees of its constitution and the tenure of its system of *historically developed laws*, to be governed as a Christian nation. Our nation has *historic rights*, one of which is Christian nurturing, that may not be infringed upon even by collaboration of the three branches of lawmaking. In recognition of the Christian popular interest as well as the unique national perspective that we defend, we are not begging for an *alm*. We request the chambers and the crown to maintain, not as a favour but as a right, the most precious national freedoms, paid for with the blood of our ancestors and grafted indelibly in our national history and then transferred identifiably to the constitution."[26]

E. NETHERLANDIC STATE STRUCTURE

Not only in maintaining freedom of conscience has the Netherlandic sense of freedom displayed itself, in our state structure this unique character can be identified too. The first connects with the other. Because of its unique Christian-Protestant nature, "our nation has its own principles, including its *state jurisprudence*." Considering other Protestant countries, "the Netherlands enjoyed a significant advantage in being rooted in *Calvinism*, adopted from France and Switzerland. In its Puritan steadfastness and resilience, she rooted her principles not just in the reformation of the church but also in the formation of the original provinces. Therefore, she is known to have original liberty, the *sine qua non* of a real constitutional government, in popular essence *national*."[27]

Calvinism has appropriately been credited with "the origin of real constitutional jurisprudence...to know its tie to God's laws for the rights of its citizens regardless of its type of government."[28]

Neither absolutism nor popular democracy are *national* to the Netherlands. But *popular input* is. "The Netherlands is a country with freedom in which the rights of special people and corporations of all kinds are respected. When not administered under the yoke of aristocrats, popular input was important in the decisions concerning state issues. Considerable contributions of the citizens are not only constitutional, but express a Netherlandic principle."[29]

It is also evident in the nature of the kingdom as it was formed after 1813 [which marks the end of the French occupation under Napoleon Bonaparte. HB] "Here royalty, likely more than in any other country, has been steeped with

91

BUILDING A NATION ON ROCK OR SAND

republican understanding and spirit. It has a republican root because it is perceived out of the history of the original provinces. The king is the eminent head,
which the nation always coveted. In this simple truth hides the guarantee against
sidestepping one way or the other. In the Netherlands, the king is not an aristocrat nor a puppet...but rather its protector of the popular rights and freedoms.
Sometimes if necessary he protects against pressure of the majority, other times
against a temporary opinion. With this understanding, in 1813, the title *sovereign*
was not dangerous because it found its correction in popular history."

Misunderstanding was hardly possible "because the king and the people
understood that this land had been liberated from the Spanish aristocrat and
they would defend it against any repeat...No other structure of their state would
be possible than the one based on its own unique popular history, steeped with
republican essence and spirit."[30]

This sovereignty did "not allow revolutionary autocracy...no unlimited
authority in the way it is exercised nor in the structures in which it operates.
No limiting of popular freedom and input until there is barely room left for it;
no random and meticulous regulating of issues that are not tied to governing
practices."[31]

Therefore, Groen could declare, in spite of the fact that he disliked the word
democracy since at that time it was almost synonymous to sovereignty of the people or popular sovereignty, "I appreciated an element of democracy, *popular
input*, because of our history, or popular sovereignty. I consider it a precious and
probably an indispensable element in the *Netherlandic constitutional* state
structure."[32] In the Second Chamber, this influence could be applied.

Did Groen see possible shortcomings of the parliamentary system? He
repeatedly warned against the abuse of power in the Second Chamber. It had to
abide within the limits of its granted power in order not to endanger the independence of the authority of government. "Everywhere, but especially in the
Netherlands, personification of state supremacy must be seen as anti-national
application of its state jurisprudence. Nor should one subject the authority of
the king to the power of the parties in the Chamber, which all defenders of royal
authority readily support." He did not want to "see a gold-plated rooster on the
steeple, which, from its exceptionally lofty and grand position, fails to observe
the political whims and consequently to point them out. Now without imagery,
no figurehead king only who, in maintaining freedom of conscience and
dissolving of conscience subjection, would be powerless."[33]

Groen was not prepared to throw the whole system overboard because of a few possible excesses. He once wrote in *The Netherlander,* "One could ask: what benefit does the nation expect from the system of so-called popular representation? Such questions were already being posed. In a lesser degree (in spite of the loud voices of a few) for the scorn regarding direct elections, but the disdain for parliamentary busyness and indecisiveness in general. The pitiful leaning toward Bonapartism, the desire for a forceful government that would not be opposed in parliament and only uphold the constitutional government in form and pretense. This understandable change toward the liberal theory gets increasingly more support in the Netherlands.

"One need not worry in this regard about the anti-revolutionary position. In case direct elections were even less desirable, we do not seek the prosperity of our nation in the constant change of recently altered systems. It rather lies in the revival of the national spirit, which is never revealed better than in the victory over anti-national laws.

"Enervation and denervation of the Netherlandic parliament deserves lament, not rejoicing. What would be the consequence? Autocracy and bureaucracy. We don't desire to see parliament first get excited about revolutionary extremism of false theories and then during disappointment become subjected to unprincipled reactions and exclusively to material interests and administrative rule. The attitude in parliament needs to be undeniably connected to the rights and freedoms of the nation."[34] Whenever parliament meets that criteria, natural consultation between government and parliament guarantees freedom and authority. It provides healthy popular input.

Parliament needs to acknowledge its responsibility, especially in demonstrating "those main principles that shape governing and lawmaking.

"This is desirable, including for government itself, since in the House the heartbeat of the nation should be evident. Yes, to me, debating the main principles is a necessary and excellent calling of elected members of the House. If their task lay mostly or solely in the application of laws, a better system of government should be chosen. The constitutional parliamentary system may be considered the least desirable then. The positive and often undervalued privilege of this form of government is that the interests, desires and feelings of the population can be expressed. It allows a place for steady general consultation and debate between government and nation. This system only affords continuing and meaningful popular input in the affairs of the nation."[35]

Government needs to abstain from interference, which is not part of its competence. No central regulating, but the independence of the parts, of social and cultural bodies, promote healthy national development. "What does independence mean in this context? I don't have any simpler answer than *independence in its own sphere*. Independence outside of its sphere can happen to a great extent with subjection and dependence; inside its sphere there has to be independence if people desire to maintain self-determination."

"Independence in the family means that the father does not receive instructions concerning his family; yet in the community, the family is subjected to the municipal government. Self-determination in each sphere yet in subjection to the whole is the *conditio sine que non* of a well-organized state. The state needs to be a composition of parts that each have identity, peculiarity and acquired rights, which do not allow them to be subjected to state authority."[36]

In all his political and juridical activities, Groen remained faithful to these principles. He concisely formulated the purpose of his anti-revolutionary politics as follows: "We wanted to put aside the liberal theories by practicing Christian, historic, Netherlandic principles.

"Following 1848, we did not want a reaction of conservatism, which meant suffocation of liberty and dousing of the popular spirit by smartly taking back that which had been granted. It is more important to consider the contemporary scene by sticking to and possibly improving the constitution. Maintaining a government by the grace of God and by His will as well as the naturally developed laws of the land is preferred over the arbitrary approval by the popular majority. Supporting a king who governs with a responsible cabinet is a better choice. A cabinet that acts independently based on listening and conviction is an excellent instrument for wellbeing and a desirable defense against abuse of the royal office. The king is not a figurehead nor an autocrat. The cabinet provides informed leadership while the House exercises oversight and the privilege to veto. No significant change in the way of governing should happen without popular consultation. No rejection of the government budget is acceptable as an option to force one's way. It dissolves the state structure into the majority of the House and of the electorate. No systematic licentiousness should be chosen but rather the authority guaranteed by a mutually bonding liberty: freedom of conscience; freedom of worship; freedom to organize; freedom of education; freedom to exercise rights; and above all, freedom of everything connected to taking responsibility."[37]

F. COOPERATION AND ISOLATION

Maintaining this national inheritance was an important condition for the well-being of the Netherlandic spirit, and therefore Groen considered it the foundation of a Netherlandic political program. He saw it as the basis of cooperation for all those well-disposed. But that cooperation had to be established because "the most important condition of our national strength is unity among people of the same nation."[38]

However, unity and unity can differ, since not *every* unity is positive toward reaching that determined goal. Groen had many opportunities to express his thoughts on this subject. Repeatedly people criticized him that his principles were too exclusive to promote cooperation. "You place yourself apart," people pointed out to him, "and instead of promoting cooperation, you disturb it."

Especially around 1848 this question was raised. The liberals particularly praised the spirit of unity that had prevailed during the revision of the Netherlandic constitution. People pointed to the division and civil unrest that had ripped apart other European nations during that year of revolution.

Groen felt it a duty to examine this highly praised unity more closely and to demonstrate in detail his rejection of this view. The results of his examination have been preserved in a stocky document entitled *Grondwetherziening en Eensgezindheid* (Constitutional Revision and Unity).

Here he identifies various kinds of unity. He mentions, for example, "a *forced* unity. The dominance of one group or the fear of another group can be so strong that no effort in opposing it takes place. This type of unity shows itself in subjection and passivity, in an oppressive and sorry manner." It surfaced obviously and broadly in the Netherlands during the reign of Napoleon.

Groen also identified a *damaging* unity. "It is possible in deed and with complete conviction to unite together to gain for some or everyone that which is damaging and depraved. Wherever a depraved unity exists, the dissolution of unity is desirable. Unity formed out of disunity, established out of a devotion to duty is one way to have a desirable unity as a virtuous basis...Breaking up such a conflict-based unity becomes a duty, since it is usually founded on devotion, which opens the way to establish desirable unity on a sound foundation. It is not commendable to remain silent for the sake of unity without any examination of its meaning and value."[39]

Groen became convinced through his investigation that the unity in 1848 was not genuine. He found that a small, energetic minority "under the pressure of assumed irresistibility of an ultraliberal opinion traceable to the victory in Paris" caused the constitutional revision to yield to liberal theories that were not desirable to the whole nation. "In reality the general mindset did not match the liberal one; most people did not understand the points of difference; the majority of the politically astute people did not appreciate, even dislike, these sizable and corrupt changes."

This observation led Groen to question how this minority managed to realize its intentions and consequently introduced a period of liberal dominance. "The answer," according to Groen "lies in the fact that some in high (political) positions speak forcefully, which makes the majority willing to listen and be silent. It is natural to lean toward new ideas. Demanding any kind of concessions is considered state-like gymnastics.

"People hoped to sidestep socialism by agreeing to points that at first were refused as radicalism. In revolutionary times, a considerably small minority can promote its desire as the generally accepted desire, its view as the generally accepted view, its way as the generally accepted way. By overriding and influencing the central governing authority, it is able to subject the nation to its yoke. Fear essentially magnifies things."

Many people defended their attitude in 1848 like this: "Resistance, with the hope of winning, did not make sense. Why vain display? For what reason harmful colliding? Why not rather willingly cooperate with things done against our will and praise? Wasn't it the law that demanded of the Christian citizens to unite in offering their helping hand to establish that which could no longer be stopped?"[40]

Over against this "so-called, this forced, this damaging, this depraved unity by which people out of despondency and fearing the victory of the opposition, joined them under their banner,"[41] Groen posed a unity of a completely different kind. Its characteristics are in line with our own principles and observing our national traditions.

The unity, accomplished by the revolutionaries, is the unity of being unprincipled. Therefore "when unity cannot be achieved by means of unity of principles then unity becomes the surrogate unity; then order has to be created by complete submission to government."[42] This kind of unity, identified by abandoning principles, was opposed by Groen's well-known slogan: *in our isolation lies our strength*.

Groen objected when people interpreted it as an endeavour to seclusion and an impediment to cooperation. Groen explained this slogan like this: "In aversion to the boldness of the numerical majority, I don't mean to go as far as to suggest that our strength lies in the numerical minority. Others suggest that this slogan encourages hedging and political hermitage, which makes the leader of this unique movement strictly faithful to his fanciful view and confined to his own demarcated camp as a lonesome warrior. This maxim has a more reasonable explanation. We have our own indispensable principle, which may require me to work with a few or even alone, rather than to abandon a position to gain influence and recognition as a party. In our isolation, our consistency with principle, we have strength. Strength to pose resistance to anyone who tries to push us from our foundation. Strength to draw those who come destitute and sympathetic. We repeat loud and clearly: *In our isolation* (when consistent in principle, we may even be left alone) *lies our strength*. This strength works two ways: it repels and attracts."[43]

Groen's position was supple enough that he would negotiate within principle consistency for concessions to bring about unity. He realized that in times of danger, disagreements, which usually controlled relationships and which by themselves were important, needed to be put on hold or set aside. Untiringly, he fought with conservatives, Roman Catholics and liberals. In 1865, he did not refrain from writing this: "In all of Europe as well as in our homeland, questions are raised that probe religion, rights and morality. These questions put the divisions of Catholic and Protestant, liberal and conservative, and even Thorbeckian and anti-Thorbeckian party in the background."[44]

When in 1848 our country was endangered, too, by the revolution, Groen formulated his points, underlying cooperation, more precisely. He did not take a narrow approach: "With an uncertain future, especially now that the Netherlands is being threatened by immeasurable dangers inside and outside, there is no defense unless the well-disposed come to a mutual disposition and general consultation concerning it."

"The best solution, which seems impossible to me—unity of all on the foundation, which I and my fellow believers and friends believe is impossible but hold essential and essential to move forward. But, considering that the most desirable goal cannot be reached does not mean that we should avoid a second-best solution: namely uniting the well-disposed based on free choice cooperation guided by everyone's own position, each according to their own belief and insight in regard to godliness, morality, obtained rights and national independence. In short a unity around all those valued views, in opposition to the monstrously delusive wisdom of the day, treasured by thoughtful and brave citizens in the Netherlands. To build such a unity, more than ever under the current situation, requires mutual tolerance and mutual respects for each other's convictions. It does not tolerate forceful imposition of ideas on everyone, whether supported by a few or by many, as acceptable."[45]

A few months later, Groen developed his point of view in more detail. He added this to the statement above: "It should be clear that when I identify the *well-disposed*, I do not limit myself to friends and fellow believers. I do not hold those as well-disposed who feel comfortable with my point of view. Such strictness is less advisable now and unreasonable in our times. There is so much confusion with the many points of view right now. It is a time in which ambitious promoters claim ideas they do not understand themselves. Many are not familiar with the nature and the essence of their party that they have enthusiastically chosen to support. It is not unusual that a clear tension is revealed between the arguments of the mind and the feelings of the heart. I am exceptional but in a different way than people usually accuse me. By conviction a Christian, I declare that the denial of the gospel is and remains the cause of all evils that plague Europe. I view Protestantism, since its protest is built upon the unchangeable foundation of God's Word, as an inestimable blessing, especially for the Netherlands. While some suggest it represents a narrow mindset or steadfast conviction, I pose that a broad perspective and a loving tolerance can be paired. Without leaving my conscience-founded point of view or making truth, which is beyond my decision making, a topic of negotiation, and without overlooking the differences that exist between me and others, I can now concentrate on the agreements. I can appreciate now everything that is good and noble by intention and character. I can offer my hand honestly to the Roman Catholic and the Jew. I can offer my hand to those who claim to be conservative, liberal or even radical. It is crucial to know when I can trust or at least not have to doubt that they are rooted in the conviction of their conscience to that which is good and true and are readily available to offer their service; when they are committed to the wellbeing of the homeland, and everybody according to their own belief and understanding are committed to participate in the struggle to safeguard the sacred human heritage. False prophets of today, with theories not developed from other worldly sources, threaten in desperation. Well-disposed and an ally to me is everyone, without distinction of religious or political confession, who

98

is dedicated to the protection of the foundations of society. It takes a mutual approach, acquainting, trust and consultation. There needs to be an honest desire and attempt for mutual consultation....

"The anti-revolutionary party, since it is founded upon the truth, respects all that is true and good in the diverse directions. Despite the intolerance of the Church of Rome, we grant it rights and freedoms in good faith because of comparing it with other denominations. We rejoice over everything in that church that opposes unbelief and reflects a precious evangelical witness. Even though the anti-revolutionaries reject the conservative system, they praise the followers of preservation for their desire to resist the theories of falsehoods. The anti-revolutionaries cannot fault the followers of the revolution their desire for freedom, even when they regret that they will never know the nature and the conditions for true freedom. They recognize among all dispositions followers of goodwill, despite the difference in mindset, who defend religion, rights, freedom and order and offer directly or indirectly important services in society."[46]

G. PRINCIPLES AND PARTIES

It is clear that Groen, from his point of view, did not consider the dismantling of political parties a condition for unity. If oneness is possible, it certainly would "not happen by denying the existence of parties or by putting them in a bad light." Groen accepted "that the establishment of political parties was unavoidable as soon as there appeared interest in public issues and diversity of views." When others challenged him with an ideal example without such groupings, he replied, "We object only to this seductive system in as far as a government is fallible. Its policies and political behaviour need review and checks. It is the reason we consider parties (a systematic distinction of political views) a necessity and a privilege in a constitutional system of government."[47]

Once Groen commented to Thorbecke in the Second Chamber, "He has made me a black sheep with a bad habit when I speak about *my party;* he never refers to his *party!* The reason is that his party—confirmed by the history of earlier liberal governments—dislikes government based on parties. They would rather nationalize the parties and melt them together into *one* party—the liberal party, which no longer would be a party but would be referred to as the nation." During another instance, a member of the Chamber bragged that he was no party man. Groen replied: "I definitely am a party man! In the struggle for principles, which divide Europe and the Netherlands, I have made a choice: to dedicate my life in defense of principles."[48]

There is a difference between parties and partisanship. Partisanship is not based on the difference of principles but is revealed in personal and material considerations. It shines in disparaging its opponent with abusive and impeaching attacks. Groen disliked this battle approach because he fought for and with principles. His opposition to the first Thorbecke cabinet and other principled views he explained like this: "If ever, but certainly not in these days, is opposition fitting when based on false ambition, pride, vanity, repressible ties to the previous government, dislike for persons or difference of individual opinions."

"No other opposition is worthy than the one that is rooted in principles; only, if I may say so, a systemic opposition. That kind is not against people, but against principles. It may be tied to respect for talents, intentions and even the character of others, whose falsehoods I regret and actions I cannot appreciate."[49] This attitude raises the party debate to a higher plane. By exposing the intentions of the opponent fairly, it is possible in times of danger to join together for the sake of the country. "When are parties, which are indeed considered indispensable, not a danger to the state? Only when without losing their party identity they reach out to each other for a higher patriotic reason." It should be understood that difference in party does not have to mean a difference in patriotism. "Love of country rises above difference of views."

H. THE HEART OF THE NATION

Groen counted with significant confidence on possible cooperation, since he posed the Anti-Revolutionary Party (ARP) as a national party. One of its most important characteristics was of course "that it was *bound to the faith of its ancestors and their history by tradition.*" When people commented to him that he was "leader of a *fraction of the nation,*" he responded, "This fraction is more than a fragment. It is—bound to popular faith and popular history—the heart of the nation. The Reformed character of our people is the life source of the Netherlandic state. Our fraction cannot be minimized by ultramontane criticism nor by liberal self-conceit. This fraction has opposed unbelief and superstition from the sixteenth to the nineteenth century. It is rooted steadfastly in the teaching of the Reformation and is alive on this Protestant martyrs' soil.

"In that connection, I dare to claim the title *popular leader*. Whether member of the Second Chamber or not, I claim to be a *people's representative*. One could call me the representative of the *Netherlandic* people in as much as it appreciates its popular history, especially those most glorious periods, and its popular faith, which was the cement of the early republic and still confesses its only comfort in life and death."[52]

Groen never despaired for the survival of this heart of the nation that even during long-time rule under revolutionary theories remained untainted. "I trust that in spite of all tests by political specialists and anatomists there remains a nation with an essential being that does not dissolve in constitutional rules. Its life has continued under previous forms of government. It has not lost its understanding of religion, truth and rights. It remembers the contributions of its ancestors and appreciates the essence and source of these contributions that tore other countries. It does not expect its guidance for its own thoughts and behaviour from levity or frenzy of parties. It does not equalize the promotion of the victory of a party that has brought about various troubles to the nation during the last sixty years with the fulfillment of national wellbeing.

"Am I concluding too much when claiming that many citizens display the popular national characteristics in their action and their walk, such as calm consideration, diligence, dislike for rioting, submission to God and the established government among the upper and the lower class, among tradespeople as well as those well off?

"Thankfully there are people in every grouping to whom duty, faithfulness, bravery is no idle talk. They understand submission for the sake of conscience. They desire freedom not as a cover to anger but by being devoted to duty and responsibility. They recognize every patriotic ideal and treasure it in their heart. Among these people do I search for a patriotism that rises above the current times and forms the heart and the strength of the Netherlandic people. This nation rooted in its historic soil remains itself despite all the changes that occur."[53]

Groen felt an intimate connection with this national heart. It offered him strength even though its influence appeared much diminished at that time. Once when others spoke of him and his fellow workers in the Second Chamber as a small party, he said, "Is our party small? Yes. However, watch out to minimize its proper image, which could mislead people. Are we a political party? Yes! We have our own principles embedded in its jurisprudence. However, considering the usual political presence, we are not influential. Our strength is not found there.

"To make myself clearer, I may use a quote, found in an international daily newspaper after the election of 1852, which really struck a chord with me: 'Even though a member of the anti-revolutionary party is banned from the chamber or not, it is indisputable that the number of devout that form most of the anti-revolutionary party has surprisingly increased during the most recent years. It is a party that in its treatment of public issues is worth watching.' With this meaningful epithet, *the devout,* it is pinpointed where our strength can be identified; the *devout* with whom politics connects with the faith and history of the nation (1 Peter 5:1-11). The small party can be strong too. The results of our policy can be understood in church and school, among all classes of people. There is a tie that binds the least to the same foundation of peace for the soul and the same motivation of devotion to duty and responsibility.

"More than a popular whim or a passing enthusiasm, this conversation or rather this confession resounds in the consciousness and the conscience, the *Christian conscience of the Netherlandic people.*"[54]

EPILOGUE

Your Nation's Example

TOPICS WITH QUESTIONS
(HARMEN BOERSMA)

" **W**hat does Groen van Prinsterer tell us today?" was the question Smitskamp put to the Netherlandic people in this, his most popular publication. It had been over seventy-five years since Groen had formulated his principles. It has been almost seventy-five years since Smitskamp collected and arranged Groen's ideas into this concise format.

The "pernicious" ideas of the French Revolution were not unfamiliar to Canadian Christians before the nation of Canada was formed. Is it not a good time to collect and reflect upon the principles that have shaped this young nation? What are these founded upon? Others have documented stories about the leaders of our country.

As one of the preferred destinations in the world for immigration, Canada has a greater variety of people and backgrounds than the Netherlands did in Groen's time. Enlarging Canadian democracy with the adoption of a policy of multiculturalism, the Canadian solution will likely turn out differently. In that sense, democracy continues to be an experiment.

If your citizenship is with another nation, how do these questions and ideas shape the story of traditional and national development of your nation? What rules the heart of your people?

To get an understanding of the spirit of the nation is a complicated quest. It requires taking the "temperature" of many issues. Consider the following list

103

of topics, the leading questions, and the additional resources for discussion in your group as a guide with your nation's example:

1. **Biographies and autobiographies** are helpful documentations to gain understanding of a person's life. Smitskamp kept his biography of Groen brief. For a more detailed biography, consult *Groen van Prinsterer: His Life and Work* by Gerrit J. Schulte.[1] Other recommended works in the context of this work: *Witness to Hope* by George Weigel.[2] It follows Pope John Paul II in detail. *Think Big* by E. Preston Manning.[3] *Night* by Jewish author Elie Wiesel.[4] Which biographies have you read and appreciated? Whose biography would you like to see written or documented in a movie? Explain. Check out *Canada: Portraits of Faith,* a collection of one-page biographies with a portrait of twenty Canadians.[5]

2. **Family trees** are a popular pastime for many people. Why is knowing one's ancestors and their story important for people? How does that relate to their identity? Matthew 1 in the Bible traces the family tree or bloodline from Abraham to Jesus. How do you see the connection between this family tree and God's promise of the Saviour? Some refer to it as the "golden thread of prophecy" in the Bible. Google this term and check the interesting references on various sites. What happened to that line after Christ left the earth? Doesn't it turn into a faith line? How would you trace your heritage of faith? For example: Jesus, Apostle Paul, Augustine, Boniface, Willibrord (apostle to the Frisians), Gregory (the Great), Maarten Luther, John Calvin, Groen van Prinsterer, Abraham Kuyper, Herman Dooyeweerd, Francis Schaeffer, Billy Graham, Calvin Seerveld, R.C. Sproul. What does your faith heritage look like? How does it tie in with "the cloud of witnesses" in Hebrews 11 and 12?

3. The translator's introduction refers to families in rural communities. How may the contribution to culture of the **rural and urban** resident differ and be the same? How would you describe the benefits and the disadvantages of rural and urban life? What problems do rural living and urban jobs create for families, businesses, schools, transportation, governments? What issues are current in the development of your urban area? What evidence and value do you see in efforts to make urban development "greener"? Check out *The Meaning of the City*[6] by Jacques Ellul. Explore contributions Cardus is making to city planning for Canadian cities.[7]

4. What connection exists between the Living God, the living gospel and a living faith? Is there evidence of "**the living gospel**" in our community, our country? How does it manifest itself? Is it limited to one institution, such as the church? Should it be? In which other social institutions can it be evident? How is it more personal than institutional? How does personal faith connect to communal faith? Check out leaders of revivals, e.g., Jonathan Edwards, George Whitefield[8] in the 18th century, Abraham Kuyper in the late 19th century, or American evangelists of the 20th century. Check out *Loving the City*[9] about one contemporary person's pursuit of a gospel balanced ministry. On a scale of one to ten, how important to you is this statement of Groen: "To overcome the world, it is necessary to defeat all arguments in our own heart first"? (Pg. 22.) Explain.

5. Groen discovers ideas and direction in the Bible narrative. Even though he becomes more apocalyptic in chapter two, he stays connected to daily living and events. Bible study, prayer, and fellowship are important habits to him. What is your experience with **devotional habits**? Can you share one story or incident that made this real in your life? What effect does devotion have on faith formation in a person's heart? Consult Calvin G. Seerveld's *How to Read the Bible to Hear God Speak, A Study in Numbers 22-24* and *Prayer* and *The Songs of Jesus*, both by Timothy Keller and *Operation World*.[10]

6. Other authors have shared their appreciation for the Bible. Canadian Northrop Frye wrote *The Great Code: The Bible and Literature*.[11] He argued that the Great Code of Western Christian literature has been the Bible. How do you respond to that statement? Can you support the idea that **the Bible is the foundation of Western culture**? Explain. How did Groen connect faith and politics? Explore this definition: "Culture is human action developing nature." Why can it have constructive or destructive results? What is the importance of the Canadian Bible League? How is reading the Bible and studying it with a topical approach important to culture? Check out *The Central Significance of Culture*[12] and also *The Christians: Their First Two Thousand Years*[13] by Ted Byfield. It proposes a story written with a basis of Christian civilizational principles.

7. For study of the Bible, it is important to own a good **Bible version**.
   a) The Orthodox disciple may turn to *The Orthodox Study Bible*,[14] which appeared as recently as 2016. Its subtitle is *Ancient Christianity Speaks to*

Today's World. The OT is a fresh translation and the NT uses the New King James Version (NKJV). Commentaries are drawn from the ancient Christian perspective of the church fathers. "A Bible for the soul."

b) The Roman Catholic faithful may consider *The Navarre Bible.*[15] It is the Revised Standard English Version with commentaries and the New Vulgate Latin version. The three texts match content on each page.

c) The Protestant believer has various choices but may be served with the recent *Reformation Study Bible.*[16] It uses the Revised Standard Version for the Bible text and study notes that express consistently the Reformed perspective found in the Reformed confessions.

d) The Evangelical Christian may choose the NKJV Nelson Study Bible[17] with explanatory verse notes on each page as well as topical explanatory pages.

These are suggestions only, and believers may find it helpful to cross reference text and notes from different traditions. A very effective way is a small study group in which each person or couple contributes from a different Bible (tradition). If one is able to draw together a small study group, adherents from each tradition may be the ultimate mix for a deep and rich devotional, worship, and learning environment. How may this type of Bible study affect the "spirit of the times"?

8. The **church** was one institution that drew Groen's attention. As empires crumbled into smaller nations, so the church split into smaller units. As church and empire governments competed or cooperated in the Middle Ages, now national governments legalized state churches. Groen spoke out for the free development of churches. Detailed in *The Miracle of the Nineteenth Century: About Free Churches and Common People* (only in Dutch) is the development and spread of new churches in and from countries of the Reformation. Check out a concise church history, e.g., *Church History: The Rise and Growth of the Church in its Cultural, Intellectual and Political Context.*[18]

9. With such a variety of Christian denominations and world religions represented in our country, how can they all have a voice in **the nation's political system**? What solution did Groen offer? How did Groen connect the Bible and politics? In this regard, what was the greatest disappointment for

Groen in his political career? What value would a Christian political party offer in our country? What changes in the electoral system would make that easier? How can citizens of various world religions cooperate in political parties? Is it desirable and necessary? What are your thoughts about a political creed? Try to formulate one together. Check out *Christians in the Crisis: Towards Responsible Citizenship.*[19]

10. Groen considered **the traditional family** an important institution of society. What important contributions does such a type of family contribute to the well-being of a nation? How does the Bible narrative value families? How is the past and the future of a nation connected to traditional families? Why is lawful protection of such families important? What are the causes and effects of marital breakdown in our society? Check out *What Is a Family?*[20]

11. Groen dedicated much of his time to the **education system**. He proposed a national Christian school system. Considering that education has been a high priority in the Christian heritage, how can such a system work in a pluralistic society? What experiences and solutions have been followed in our nation? Who was Egerton Ryerson, and what role did he have in establishing a public education system in Ontario, Canada? Why were separate schools established and funded here? Would public funding for a Christian education system, kindergarten to university, be discriminatory to non-Christian citizens? How would such schools contribute to the public good? How can citizens and government both support such a system? Check out John Amos Comenius, organizer of a Protestant school system in Poland and elsewhere in the 17th century. Review the Cardus Surveys of Education. How important would a continuous Christian education system, from kindergarten to university, be for our nation?

12. **Nations and their leaders** are constantly in the news. Where does the concept of *nation* come from? Make a list of nations mentioned in the Bible. Explore each continent for its nations. Does the number of nations surprise you? Why is there so much intrigue among nations? Why are nations constantly in flux? What effect does this have on people? What effect does the movement of people (immigrants, refugees) across boundaries have? What benefits and difficulties concern you with the idea of governments tracking people? What spiritual purpose may exist for nations?

Check out *Operation World*[21] and *Abraham Kuyper: Modern Calvinist, Christian Democrat.*[22]

13. Which **public documents (charters)** can you identify that seem like a social contract between people and governments? Who initiated them? How does that origin differ from the *Magna Carta* or *The Great Charter of Liberties* signed by King John in England in 1295? What do they offer? Do they proclaim rights or responsibilities? What is the difference? Why does it matter in reviewing Groen's story? Do they make our understanding and our love for country stronger? If our country is a unique, naturally formed nation, do we really need such contracts or charters? How does a charter differ from a political creed?

14. How would you **characterize Canada** (or your country) **as a nation**? What founded our country? Can these principles qualify as universal ones? How are they being internalized? What responsibility do the home, the school, the state, the faith community, the media and others have in the social architecture? If only one is responsible, which one would you choose? Why? What role do values have in the formation of a nation? Are values the same as principles? Check out the article "Canadian Values and Charlottetown."[23]

15. Groen suggested that the basic freedom defended by the Netherlandic people was **the freedom of conscience**. How does that connect with a person's convictions, conversion, testimony, struggle, suffering and victory? What other connections can you identify? Who and what offers strength, courage, determination, survival, healing, vision or other value? Can you share a story related to these values? To what "line in the sand" would you defend this freedom? How far would you go in defending it for or with someone else? How does freedom of conscience affect your marriage, family, school, business, vote, media choices, citizenship, etc.?

16. If spiritual questions and answers are important to you, how would you formulate them? Have you considered **faith formation** in your life, family, or community? How does regular worship contribute to it? What value do you see in studying creeds, confessional statements, and catechisms? How does it enhance or hinder citizenship in your view? How does it relate to "our citizenship is in heaven" (Philippians 3:20)?

17. Groen suggested that every nation has its own **unique character**. How can one start to identify it? How does the aboriginal past and present belong to our story in Canada? What are good practices to integrate diverse people into one nation? How does democracy play an important role in this integration? How can government and citizens both contribute to this integration?

18. Groen's voting supporters were identified as the common, working people. He commented that these folk had not yet been influenced by liberal, revolutionary ideas but continued to live a pious, hardworking lifestyle. What is the important connection between **work/labour** and citizenship? How do devout citizens benefit a nation? What important service have unions provided for workers? Check out *The Guide*, magazine of the Christian Labour Association of Canada.

19. The Solid Foundation, Chapter 5, ends with a rhymed version of Psalm 33 on a Genevan Psalter tune. The **150 rhymed psalms** were translated from French into Dutch by Petrus Datheen on the same Genevan melodies in 1566. In 1773 they were rhymed anew and in use until 1938. Therefore the Genevan Psalter has been used in worship in the Reformed churches in the Netherlands for four centuries. Musical selections in Reformed worship vary from the Genevan Psalter to contemporary evangelical songs. Trace the musical development in your church worship style. What unique quality comes with the Genevan Psalter tunes in terms of the scales in which they are composed? How does that affect the mood of the psalm? How does it affect the mood of the congregation? Compare this psalm tune type with the Scottish Presbyterian psalm melodies. What is the benefit of keeping these traditions going and what benefit could change offer to church worshippers? Trace the history of changes in hymn books in your or another denomination. List the year of a new hymnbook and compare the changes that occurred.

20. The **media** have an important place in public debate of national and local issues. Currently **social media** makes an important contribution to communication. What was the most important media for Groen? How effective was it considering the percentage of the population that was literate then? Comment. Has communication improved with the multiplicity of communication tools? Explain. Do you read newspapers? How much time do you reserve for it? How do you participate in public debate? Is it

effective? Have the written media lowered the standard for language? How important, do you think, is media airing news and views of a specific ethnic, religious, or other social group? Explain.

21. The Netherlands went through two occupations: the French Period (1795-1813) and the WWII-Nazi occupation (1940-1945). Groen suggested that Christianity and the revolution both have the potential to **branch out into every part of society and into every institution**. To get a sense of how this can happen concretely, there are novels that may help identify different influences and how they are "legged" by people into everyday relationships, choices, and actions. Read *The Occupied Garden*[24] and list actions from one chapter that the Nazis performed and actions that the Reformed Christians took. Compare and discuss your lists. Dig a little deeper into specifics, reread sections together, and discuss them. This exercise will help to untangle "the interwoven branches of two trees each with its own roots." Select another book from a different period and culture if you find this activity helpful. Then apply it to your own community, region or country.

Endnotes

The Dutch titles in the endnotes have been maintained the same as in Smitskamp's original to make it easier for those who know Dutch to expand their own research in the original documents.

INTRODUCTION TO THE ENGLISH TRANSLATION

1. Hendrik Smitskamp, *Wat Heeft Groen van Prinsterer Ons Vandaag te Zeggen?* p. 23 (in *Building a Nation*...p.26, 27)
2. H. and A. Algra, *Dispereert Niet: Twintig Eeuwen Historie van de Nederlanden, 5 Volumes.* Uitgeverÿ T. Wever, Franeker. Vol. 3 p.128.
3. Francis A. Shaeffer, *How Should We Then Live? The Rise and Decline of Western Thought and Culture.* Fleming H. Revell Company, Old Tappan, New Jersey, USA. 1976. p.120 ff, "The Enlightenment."
4. Hendrik Algra, *Het Wonder van de Negentiende Eeuw. Over Vrije Kerken en Kleine Luyden.* Uitgevery van Wijnen, Netherlands. 2003.
5. Harry Van Dyke, *Unbelief and Revolution*, Lecture XI. Amsterdam, 1973, p. v
6. Ibid, p. vii

CHAPTER 1

1. *Ongeloof en Revolutie*, 5th edition, p. 406
2. *Verscheidenheid over staatsregt en politiek*, p. 86; *Ongeloof en Revolutie*, p. 345
3. *Adviezen in de Tweede Kamer der Staten-Generaal*, part I, p. 149
4. Ibid, part II, p. 10
5. Correspondence between Groen van Prinsterer and Dr. Kuyper, p. 358

6. *Nederlandsche Gedachten*, series II, part V, p. 255
7. Ibid, part V, p. 346
8. Ibid, part I, pp. 213, 221
9. Ibid, part I, p. 302; part II, p. 348
10. Ibid, part I, p. 301

CHAPTER 2

1. *Nederlandsche Gedachten*, series II, part II, pp. 348ff
2. Ibid, series III, part III, p. 116
3. *Verscheidenheid over staatsregt en politiek*, p. 351
4. *Nederlandsche Gedachten*, series I, part III, p. 64
5. *Narede van vijfjarige strijd*, p. 115
6. *Nederlandsche Gedachten*, series II, part I, p. 316
7. *Verscheidenheid over staatsregt en politiek*, pp. 331, 335
8. *Handboek*, paragraph 1105
9. *Adviezen*, part I, pp. 47ff
10. *Verspreide Geschriften*, part I, p. 321
11. *Ongeloof en Revolutie*, p. 385
12. *Verspreide Geschriften*, part I, pp. 322ff
13. *Handboek*, p. ix
14. *Proeve over de middelen waardoor de waarheid wordt gekend en gestaafd*, 2nd print, p. 29
15. *Handboek*, p. ix
16. *Ongeloof en Revolutie*, p. 381

CHAPTER 3

1. *Ter nagedachtenis van Stahl*, p. 29
2. Ibid, p. 27
3. *Ongeloof en Revolutie*, p. 155
4. Ibid, p. 12; *Verspreide Geschriften*, part II, p. 297 (translated from French)
5. *Ongeloof en Revolutie*, p. 158
6. Ibid, pp. 81, 99
7. Ibid, p. 159
8. Ibid, p. 164, 166
9. *Handboek*, paragraph 589.
10. *Ongeloof en Revolutie*, p. 63, 120ff
11. *Verscheidenheid over staatsregt en politiek*, p. 73

11. *Ongeloof en Revolutie,* p. 173ff
13. Ibid, p. 176 v.
14. (Was endnote 21 in the original) *Ongeloof en Revolutie,* p. 309
15. (Was endnote 14 in the original) *Grondwetherziening en Eensgezindheid,* p. 109ff
16. Ibid, p. 109ff
17. *Ongeloof en Revolutie,* p. 215ff
18. Ibid, pp. 216ff 187ff
19. Ibid, p. 19
20. *Adviezen,* part I, p. 12; *Handboek,* paragraph 831

CHAPTER 4

1. *Ongeloof en Revolutie,* pp. 307-310
2. Ibid, pp. 294, 235, 290ff
3. Ibid, p. 197
4. *Grondwetherziening en Eensgezindheid,* p. 188
5. *Ongeloof en Revolutie* p. 160ff
6. Ibid, p. 206
7. *Verscheidenheden over staatsregt en politiek,* p. 172ff
   The so-called September laws, directed at revolutionary movements and expressions, were composed and approved in 1835 by the French King Louis-Philippe, who could claim his throne thanks to a revolution.
8. *Ongeloof en Revolutie,* p. 207ff
9. Ibid, p. 344
10. *Narede van vijfjarigen strijd* (Speech to assess five year battle), p. 163
11. *Grondwetherziening en Eensgezindheid,* p. 69ff in *Nederlandsche Gedachten,* series I, part III, p. 163
12. Ibid, p. 71ff, 338; *Ongeloof en Revolutie,* p. 394ff
13. *Verspreide Geschriften,* part I, p. 188ff
14. *Ongeloof en Revolutie,* pp. 353, 350
15. *Adviezen,* part I, p. 14
16. *Nederlandsche Gedachten,* series II, part IV, pp. 161, 220
17. *Parliamentaire Studien en Schetsen,* series I, number XI, p. 16ff; *Grondwetherziening en Eensgezindheid,* p. 69
18. *Handboek,* paragraph 918
19. *Nederlandsche Gedachten,* series II, part I, p. 76; *Verspreide Geschriften,* part II, p. 249ff

20. *Adviezen,* part II, p. 249ff
21. *Aan G. Graaf Schimmelpenninck,* pp. 34, 40ff
22. *Nederlandsche Gedachten,* series II, part IV, p. 275

CHAPTER 5

1. *Ongeloof en Revolutie,* pp. 17ff, 163
2. *Grondwetherziening en Eensgezindheid,* pp. 334, 352
3. *Adviezen,* part I, p. 15
4. *Ongeloof en Revolutie,* pp. 43-48
5. Ibid, pp. 132ff, 144ff
6. *Verscheidenheden over staatsregt en politiek,* p. 101
7. *Verspreide Geschriften,* part I, p. 251
8. *Handboek,* paragraphs 826a, 826
9. *Ongeloof en Revolutie,* p. xxxiiff

CHAPTER 6

1. *Handboek,* paragraph 1101
2. *Ongeloof en Revolutie,* pp. 8, 405
3. *Grondwetherziening en Eensgezindheid,* p. 449
4. *Ongeloof en Revolutie,* p. 8ff
5. Ibid, pp. 7, 9ff
6. *Handboek,* 6th edition, p. 900ff
7. *Ongeloof en Revolutie,* p. 404ff
8. Ibid, p. 401
9. *Adviezen,* part II, p. 256
10. *Nederlandsche Gedachten,* series II, part III, p. 68; *Ongeloof en Revolutie* pp. 155ff, 162
11. *Nederlandsche Gedachten,* series II, part I, p. 128; series I, part III, p. 13
12. *Adviezen,* part II, p. 299
13. *Nederlandsche Gedachten,* series II, part I, p. 318
14. *Grondwetherziening en Eensgezindheid,* p. 244ff
15. *Nederlandsche Gedachten,* series II, part II, p. 382; *Aan de Kiezers* (To the Voters), III
16. *Nederlandsche Gedachten,* series II, part I, p. 5; *Narede van vijfjarigen strijd,* p. 166ff
17. *Studien en Schetsen ter Schoolwetherziening,* p. 56; *Grondwetherziening en Eensgezindheid,* p. 329ff

18. *Ongeloof en Revolutie*, pp. 401-404
19. *Aan de Kiezers*, XX, p. 42

CHAPTER 7

1. *Nederlandsche Gedachten*, series I, part I, p. 1ff
2. *Ongeloof en Revolutie*, p. 226
3. *Adviezen*, part I, p. 357ff
4. *Narede van vijfjarigen strijd*, p. 164; *Verspreide Geschriften*, part I, p. 500
5. *Nederlandsche Gedachten*, series I, part I, p. 69
6. *Grondwetherziening en Eensgezindheid*, p. 180ff
7. *Nederlandsche Gedachten*, series II, part I, p. 1
8. *Adviezen*, part I, p. 46
9. *Verspreide Geschriften*, part II, p. 254ff
10. *Grondwetherziening en Eensgezindheid*, p. 481, 368ff; *Ongeloof en Revolutie*, p. 400
11. *Adviezen*, part II, p. 251
12. *Nederlandsche Gedachten*, series I, part II, p. 137
13. *Grondwetherziening en Eensgezindheid*, p. 176; *Proeve over de middelen waardoor de waarheid wordt gekend* (Proof about the means of knowing the truth), p. 74
14. *Nederlandsche Gedachten*, series 1, part III, p. 31
15. Ibid, p. 45
16. *Ongeloof en Revolutie*, p. 124
17. *Handboek,* paragraph 85a
18. *Verspreide Geschriften*, part I, p. 201; *Narede van vijfjarigen strijd*, p. 14ff
19. *Vrijheid van Christelijk-Nationaal Onderwijs*, p. 2; *Ter nagedachtenis van Stahl*, p. V
20. *Verspreide Geschriften*, part I, p. 312
21. *Adviezen*, part II, p. 309
22. Ibid, p. 327
23. *Nederlandsche Gedachten*, series II, part I, p. 3; *Verspreide Geschriften*, part II, p. 9; *Handboek*, paragraph 927
24. *Handboek*, paragraph 1075; *Adviezen*, part II, pp. 249, 247ff
25. *Nederlandsche Gedachten*, series II, part II, p. 223; *Adviezen*, part I, p. 22
26. *Vrijheid van Christelijk-National Onderwijs*, p. 11; *Adviezen*, part 11, p. 131; *Nederlandsche Gedachten*, series II, part III, p. 104
27. *Nederlandsche Gedachten*, series II, part II, p. 30

28. Ibid, p. 95; *Ongeloof en Revolutie,* p. 127

29. *Verspreide Geschriften,* part I, p. 198; *Adviezen,* part I, p. 48

30. *Adviezen,* part II, p. 173; *Handboek,* paragraph 967

31. *Verspreide Geschriften,* part I, p. 204

32. *Nederlandsche Gedachten,* series II, part IV, p. 363

33. Ibid, part I, pp. 77, 79

34. *Narede van vijfjarigen strijd,* p. 52ff

35. *Adviezen,* part II, p. 139

36. Ibid, part I, p. 340ff

37. *Ter nagedachtenis van Stahl,* p. 20ff

38. *Adviezen,* part II, p. 319

39. *Grondwetherziening en Eensgezindheid,* p. 2ff

40. Ibid, pp. 32ff, 44ff

41. *Adviezen,* part II, p. 308

42. *Ongeloof en Revolutie,* p. 207

43. *Parlementaire Studien en Schetsen,* part II, p. 336ff

44. Ibid, part I, number 1, p. 23

45. *Aan G. Graaf Schimmelpenninck,* p. 92ff

46. *Grondwetherziening en Eensgezindheid,* p. 62ff, 102

47. *Adviezen,* part I, p. 150ff; *Narede van vijfjarigen strijd,* p. 53ff

48. *Adviezen,* part I, p. 171; *Vrijheid van Christelijk-Nationaal Onderwijs,* p. 22

49. *Adviezen,* part I, pp. 11, 83

50. *Vrijheid van Christelijk-Nationaal Onderwijs,* p. 75; *Adviezen,* part II, p. 310

51. *Narede van vijfjarigen Strijd,* p. 122.

52. *Nederlandsche Gedachten,* series II, part II, p. 202ff

53. *Grondwetherziening en Eensgezindheid,* p. 253ff

54. *Adviezen,* part II, p. 132ff

EPILOGUE

1. Gerrit J. Schulte, *Groen Van Prinsterer: His Life and Work.* Translated by Harry Van Dyke. Barrhead: Inheritance Publications, 2015.

2. George Weigel, *Witness to Hope: The Biography of Pope John Paul II.* New York: HarperCollins Publishers, 1999.

3. Preston Manning, *Think Big: My Adventures in Life and Democracy.* Toronto: McClelland & Stewart, 2002.

4. Elie Wiesel, *Night.* New York: Hill & Wang, 2006.

5. Michael D. Clarke, Editor, *Canada: Portraits of Faith*. Chilliwack, BC: Reel to Real, 1998.
6. Jacques Ellul. *The Meaning of the City*. Grand Rapids, MI: Wm B. Eerdmans, 1970.
7. Cardus and the City
8. Arnold Dallimore, *George Whitefield: The life and times of the great evangelist of the 18th century revival*, 2 Volumes. London: The Banner of Truth Trust, 1970.
9. Timothy Keller, *Loving the City: Doing Balanced, Gospel-Centered Ministry in Your City*. Amazon, 2012.
10. Calvin G. Seerveld, *How to Read the Bible to Hear God Speak: A Study in Numbers 22-24*. Toronto: Tuppence Press, 2003.
   Timothy & Kathy Keller, *The Songs of Jesus*. Viking Books, 2015.
   Timothy Keller, *Prayer*. Dutton Books, 2014.
   Jason Mandryk, *Operation World: The Definitive Prayer Guide to Every Nation*. Seventh Revised Edition. Colorado Springs: Biblica Publishing, 2010.
11. Northrop Frye, *The Great Code: The Bible and Literature*. Toronto, 1981.
12. Francis Nigel Lee, *The Central Significance of Culture*. Memphis, TN: The Presbyterian and Reformed Publishing Co., 1976. (It has a select bibliography with over one hundred titles pertaining to culture.)
13. Ted Byfield, *The Christians: Their First Two Thousand Years*, 12 Volumes. Amazon, 2003.
14. *The Orthodox Study Bible: Ancient Christianity Speaks to Today's World*. Nashville, TN: Thomas Nelson, 2005.
15. *The Navarre Study Bible* with Latin and commentaries in six volumes. New York: Scepter Publishers Inc., 2005.
16. *The Reformation Study Bible* with commentaries based on a Reformed perspective. Orlando, FL: Ligonier Ministries, 1988.
17. *The Nelson Study Bible* (NKJV). Nashville, TN: Thomas Nelson, 1997.
18. Everett Ferguson, *Church History*, 2 Volumes. Grand Rapids, MI: Zondervan, 2013.
19. Gerald Vandezande, *Christians in the Crisis: Towards Responsible Citizenship*. Anglican Book Centre, 1984.
20. Edith Schaeffer, *What Is a Family*. Grand Rapids, MI: Baker House, 1975.
21. Jason Mandryk, *Operation World: The Definitive Prayer Guide to Every Nation*. Seventh Revised Edition. Colorado Springs: Biblica Publishing, 2010.

22. James D. Bratt, *Abraham Kuyper: Modern Calvinist, Christian Democrat.* Grand Rapids, MI: Wm. B. Eerdmans Publishing Co., 2013.

23. Raymond J. de Souza, "Canadian Values and Charlottetown." *Convivium Magazine*, August 2017.

24. Tracy Kasaboski and Kristen den Hartog, *The Occupied Garden: Recovering the Story of a Family in War-Torn Netherlands.* Toronto: McClelland & Stewart, 2008.

Bibliography & Additional Titles

1. Diarmaid MacCulloch, *Christianity The First Three Thousand Years.* New York: Penguin Books, 2009.

2. Christian J. Barrigar, *Freedom All The Way Up: God and the Meaning of Life in a Scientific Age.* Victoria, BC: Friesen Press, 2014

3. Alvin J. Schmidt, *Under The Influence: How Christianity Transformed Civilization.* Grand Rapids, MI: Zondervan Publishing House, 2001.

4. Charles W. Colson and Nancy Pearcey, *How Now Shall We Live?* Wheaton, IL: Tyndale House Publishers, Inc. 1999.

GROEN VAN PRINSTERER BIBLIOGRAPHY QUOTED (ALPHABETICAL ORDER)

Aan de Kiezers
Aan G. Graaf Schimmelpenninck
Adviezen in de Tweede Kamer Staten-Generaal
Archives ou Correspondence Inedite de la Maison d'Orange-Nassau
Bijdrage tot Herziening van de Grondwet: Staatshervorming in Vaderlandse Zin
Briefwisseling Groen van Prinsterer met Dr. A. Kuyper
De Nederlander
Grondwetherziening en Eensgezindheid

Handboek der Geschiedenis van het Vaderland
Narede van vijfjarige strijd
Nederlandsche Gedachten
Ongeloof en Revolutie
Parliamentaire Studien en Schetsen
Proeve over de middelen waardoor de waarheid wordt gekend
Studien en Schetsen ter Schoolwetherziening
Ter Nagedachtenis van Stahl
Verscheidenheden over staatsregt en politiek
Verspreide Geschriften
Vrijheid van Christelijk-Nationaal Onderwijs

SMITSKAMP BIBLIOGRAPHY QUOTED

Wat Heeft Groen van Prinsterer Ons Vandaag te Zeggen?

Appendix

Foreword

BY DR. HENDRIK SMITSKAMP

he intent of the publication is to explore the ideas of Groen, rather than writing about them. It answers the question in the title: "Wat heeft Groen van Prinsterer ons vandaag te zeggen?" What Can We learn from Groen van Prinsterer Today?

The publication of this document was halted by the Nazi-controlled *Rijkscommissariaat* in 1941 in spite of assurance of freedom of political opinions and views as expressed in Groen's own writings. The print-ready materials were ordered to be destroyed. One copy was suppressed. The terror of the Nazi occupation once again proved the dangers of which Groen had warned: political rudderlessness and confusion. Unbelief gives rise to revolution.

The prospectus for this original copy in 1941 stated that Groen had to search for direction at a time of change and renewal. The questions he struggled with often show a surprising similarity with those of today. Therefore it is good to still listen to him.

For the author it has been a privilege to be the intermediary in letting leaders of such exceptional stature as Groen van Prinsterer and Dr. Hendrikus Colijn still speak to the Dutch nation. The introduction was the last publication by Dr. Colijn before he was forced into Nazi captivity, from which he did not return. Their enduring wisdom and unmoving faith is sorely needed in these times.

HENDRIK SMITSKAMP (1907–1970)

His parents were Herman Smitskamp and Jannetje Adriana Ceelen, owner of a bread baking business. Hendrik married Alida Gijsberta de Gooijer in 1937, and they had three sons and one daughter. Hendrik titled his Free University dissertation *Groen van Prinsterer as Historian* (1940). In 1947, he accepted an appointment as professor in history at the Free University and declared his love for Reformed principles. Smitskamp was moulded to follow the mission of Kuyper's Free University: train Reformed scholars who practice their knowledge in society. *Wat heeft Groen van Prinsterer ons Vandaag te Zeggen?* was his most popular work, published in 1945. Smitskamp appeared to be tossed between popular or scholarly involvement. He observed, "My popular booklet about Groen and my newspaper articles pulled me into a direction I did not really want to go" (Archief-Risseeuw in VU). Soon there appeared to be limited room for his views of the past. His best contributions have been made in Netherlandic historiography and Reformed Protestantism in the nineteenth century. In his publications, Smitskamp took clear positions but did not challenge the reader to discuss them.

(Adapted from A. Th. van Deursen in
Biographical Dictionary of the Netherlands I, 1979)

Introduction

BY DR. HENDRIKUS COLIJN

Some may wonder if the ideas of a statesman who lived between 100 and 75 years ago still have any meaning for the current times with its own peculiar issues. Groen's writings deserve renewed consideration if one wants to discover the universal values of his ideas.

In the intro to the first edition of *Ongeloof en Revolutie* (*Unbelief and Revolution*), August 1847, Groen writes that there exists a natural and irrevocable connection between the two: the approach that declares human dominion over jurisprudence and scholarship/science rose out of a rejection of the gospel of Christ. Therefore, the foundation of truth and rights have been reversed. Consequently, a direction has been chosen that had to lead to idolatry and radicalism.

Rejection of the gospel will always and everywhere lead to confusion in state and society. All Groen's publications testify to this central idea, worked out in *Unbelief and Revolution:* the removal of the divine rule in the public square blurs seeing the natural and historical factors, which influence human social and civil activity. Forming and reforming, creation and recreation of society according to the discretion of humans; idolatrous obedience to the state with a centralized administration which by its own arbitrariness over property and rights, over the life and soul of the powerless population rules, is the fruit of revolutionary ideas. In contrast, Groen placed the gospel as the only workable barrier to stop the power of unbelief. He posed the gospel as the only cure to the diseases and the maladies of all times.

Has anything changed since Groen lived and the age he wrote about? Some of the outer appearances of issues may have changed. The proposals developed during the French Revolution, for example, as they were expressed in human rights or the enforcement of terror laws during the years 1792-1794, are now hardly openly defended. The terrorizing break with the past is considered conducive by few. A slow, thoughtful development is currently more supported than a sudden jump from the old to something new. Essentially, very little seems to have changed. The attitude to base all human development on human knowledge has certainly not diminished. A century ago, the recognition that God is the origin of all things seemed to be accepted in wider circles than now. Knowledge of Groen's ideas is of decisive value for those who maintain the importance of Holy Writ for public life. The Bible is still the defense against all revolutionary ideas that undermine the foundation of an ordered life.

It is exceptionally noteworthy how history has justified Groen's observations and conclusions. Like Burke and Bilderdijk, Groen became the seer who saw far into the future and therefore deserves to be heard today. It is not unusual that such seers are mocked by contemporaries as "exaggerated, untrue and hilarious." Groen defended freedom for the state, freedom for the church, freedom in education. He constantly considered the continuous development of the nation. A nation is an association of the living with those who already have died and with those who have not yet been born. The dead have left their heritage for the living, and the current generation guards the rights of those not yet born. This understanding is only saved in the womb of the gospel. Groen always affirmed openly that he was a gospel confessor.

The "seer" Groen has not been recognized by thinkers outside the Reformed circles and neither by those inside those circles. Groen is being appreciated for his contribution in history but less valued for his foundational insights and ideas. Ordinary citizens may have sensed that he made important contributions but did not grasp his thought patterns. Groen missed the gift of popularizing his ideas. One contemporary, A.F. de Savornin Lohman remarked in the foreword to the fifth edition of *Unbelief and Revolution*: "It is difficult to suppress the question: why did so many Christians ignore such a genius historian, a good citizen, a devout Christ confessor, as one reads selective quotes from his works?"

It is noteworthy that Smitskamp has been willing to republish Groen's ideas and to organize them as a unified system with a historical introduction. This makes Groen readable for a much wider public including his revolutionary opponents.

Groen was a forerunner who introduced a new era with observations and conclusions that become more valuable and increasingly more visible as they bridge a longer period.

HENDRIKUS COLIJN (1869–1944)

A Dutch statesman who as prime minister (1933–39) gained widespread popular support through his conservative anti-depression economic policies. A soldier (1895–1904) in the colonial army during the Acehnese War in northern Sumatra, Colijn later served there as a civil administrator, organizing government services and rubber plantations. He entered the Dutch parliament in 1909 as a member for the orthodox Calvinist Anti-Revolutionary Party and became war minister (1911–13). After serving as director (1914–22) of the company that later became the Royal Dutch Petroleum Company (Shell), he succeeded Abraham Kuyper in 1922 as leader of the Anti-Revolutionary Party and editor of its newspaper, *De Standaard*. He served as finance minister from 1923 to 1925. After a brief ministry in 1925–26, he became prime minister again in 1933 and pursued a policy of "adaptation" (reducing the general standard of living) and of postponing devaluation of the currency. He was forced to resign from office in July 1939 after dropping the Roman Catholic bloc from his coalition cabinet. Having remained in the Netherlands as editor of *De Standaard* after the German occupation in 1940, he was arrested in July 1941 and spent his remaining years under Nazi supervision.

(Adapted from *Encyclopedia Britannica*)

About the
Translator and Editor

Harmen Boersma was born into a family deeply rooted in the rural agricultural province of Friesland. He was raised and educated in the Gereformeerde Kerk and the Christian National school system at the elementary and secondary level. He graduated from the Christelijke Kweekschool (teacher's college) in Sneek. He also completed his compulsory military service with the armed forces of the Netherlands.

Harmen immigrated to Canada with his fiancé, Elizabeth. Here they married and raised three sons, Gerald, Harvey, Gordon and two daughters, Jeannette and Sigrid. Since moving to Canada he has taught at Drayton Christian School, Woodstock Christian School, Ottawa Christian School and served as part-time Social Studies consultant with the Ontario Alliance of Christian Schools from 1974-79. He holds a BEd from Calvin College. He also continued courses towards a MA in history at University of Western Ontario and the Institute of Christian Studies. He later changed careers to business and rebuilt myCommunity, a national community relations service. Harmen has served various church and community organizations, most consistently as a Christian Reformed Church service organist.

Harmen self-published *Treasures of Farm and Faith: First Christian Reformed Church of Kemptville: A Story of its Social and Religious Roots and Practices. Growing Towards a Reforming Catholic Christian Community* in 2015. He is currently retired and living with his wife Elizabeth in Kemptville, ON. He is still fascinated by Reformed faith and life.

Index